SCRAP CRAFTS
From McCall's Needlework and Crafts

SCRAP CRAFTS

from
McCall's
Needlework & Crafts

SEDGEWOOD™ PRESS
NEW YORK

For Sedgewood™ Press
Editorial Director, Sedgewood™ Press: *Jane Ross*
Project Director: *Wendy Rieder*
Managing Editor: *Gale Kremer*
Designer: *H. Roberts*
Production Manager: *Bill Rose*

Distributed by Meredith Corporation.

ISBN 0-696-02309-1

Library of Congress Catalog Number 83-51233

Manufactured in the United States of America

CONTENTS

INTRODUCTION

MOST PEOPLE who sew or do some kind of needlework tend to accumulate scraps of lovely fabric, embroidery floss, or yarn, which often go unused for want of appropriate projects. Many people also look for things that are relatively easy to make and inexpensive. *Scrap Crafts* answers all of these needs. It provides dozens of designs that use small amounts of fabric and other materials to create attractive and useful personal accessories, decorative accents for every part of the home, and toys and other items of special interest to children of all ages.

To satisfy divergent interests, the projects also involve a number of different sewing and needlework techniques in addition to knit and crochet and cut-and-paste work with fabric. So, no matter what your talents or proclivities, you are sure to find many appealing items on the following pages that you can make for yourself or your family or give as gifts to friends.

In the chapter "Personal and Decorative Accessories," for example, you will find a variety of fabric-covered frames, boxes, and other objects; a number of handsome pillow designs; and such interesting creations as a heart-inspired needlepoint design for framing, cachepots quilted in unusual leaf patterns, and an amusing draft stopper in the form of a parading cat family. In addition, the crafts used in that section alone include appliqué, piecing, crocheting, knitting, and a clever method of cutting and folding fabric that resembles piecing but requires only a fraction of the time.

Instructions for all the techniques used in the book are either provided with a particular project or they are given in a special section at the back of the book, along with all the embroidery stitches and the basic directions for knitting and crocheting.

Certain equipment required for making some of the projects in the book is so common that it has not been listed specifically. Such items include: pencils, colored pencils, a dry ball-point pen, a ruler, a yardstick, glue, paper-cutting scissors, and an iron. The same is true of such sewing equipment as the following: a sewing machine with a zigzag attachment, sewing and embroidery scissors, pinking shears, straight pins, sewing and embroidery needles, dressmaker's carbon, a tracing wheel, and a tape measure.

Needless to say, all of the projects in the book can be made from leftover or newly purchased materials and the colors in any of the designs can be adapted to suit your own needs. The choice of what to make is now up to you.

PART I

DRESSING UP THE KITCHEN AND TABLE

New accessories for the kitchen and table are always welcome because both areas are in constant use. For that reason, this section offers some of the most commonly needed items such as place mats and pot holders. Also included are such niceties as a pretty biscuit caddy, smart-looking appliance covers, jam jar covers for those who make preserves, charming tea cozies for tea drinkers, and a beguiling kitchen witch, who promises to bring good luck to any kitchen.

Strawberries Galore: Strawberry-inspired Accessories for Kitchen and Table

Enjoy strawberries every day of the year with any one of these colorful, coordinated projects: place mats, napkin rings, pot holders, coasters, jam jar covers, biscuit caddy, and toaster cover.

Strawberry Place Mats

SIZE: 12½″ × 17½″

MATERIALS (for 4 mats): 1 yard 36″-wide, white-dot-on-green cotton fabric; ¾ yard 36″-wide red-dot-on-white cotton; ⅛ yard 36″-wide white-dot-on-red cotton. 7 yards ⅜″-wide white-dot-on-red double-fold bias tape. Red and green sewing thread. Polyester quilt batting.

1. Making the pattern. Using pencil and ruler, draw lines across pattern connecting grid lines. Enlarge pattern by copying design on paper ruled in 1″ squares; complete pattern as indicated by dash lines. Pattern is given for left half of design; for right half, flop pattern, lining up the dash line at the center and copy, omitting berries and stems at center top and bottom. Heavy solid lines indicate positions of appliqués, fine lines position of embroidery.

2. Cutting and marking the fabric. Cut four 13½″ × 18″ pieces from red-dot-on-white fabric, white-dot-on-green fabric, and quilt batting. Set batting and white-dot-on-green lining fabric aside.

Using dressmaker's carbon and dry ball-point pen, transfer pattern to right side of red-dot-on-white pieces, but do not cut out mat. Referring to directions for *How to Appliqué* at back of book, transfer strawberry design to white-dot-on-red fabric and strawberry tops and leaves to white-dot-on-green fabric; cut out as directed.

3. Appliquéing the strawberries. Using matching thread and ⅛″-wide zigzag stitches, stitch fine embroidery lines. Align each mat with corresponding lining piece, right sides out, insert batting between them, and pin.

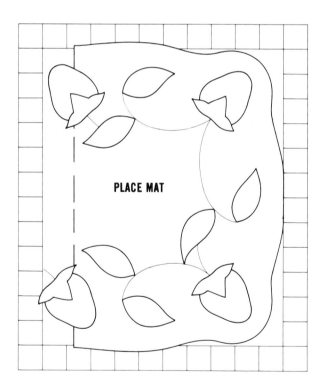

Using white thread, hand quilt around appliqués. Zigzag-stitch around mat outline, then cut out close to stitching. Enclose edge of mat with bias tape, narrow side on top, and top stitch close to inside fold through all thicknesses.

Strawberry Napkin Rings

SIZE: 2″ high

MATERIALS (for four rings): A 6½″ × 11″ piece each of white-dot-on-red and white-dot-on-green cotton fabric. A 9″ × 12″ piece of dark green felt. Polyester fiberfill. Red and green sewing thread.

1. Making the pattern. Using pencil and ruler, draw lines across napkin ring pattern to connect grid lines. Enlarge pattern by copying design on paper ruled in 1″ squares. Duplicate half patterns (indicated by dash lines) to make whole patterns.

2. Marking and cutting the fabrics. Using berry pattern, mark eight strawberries on wrong side of dotted, red fabric; cut out adding ¼″ seam allowances. Mark four strawberry tops on felt; cut out along marked lines.

3. Stitching the strawberries. Right sides together and edges aligned, stitch two strawberry pieces together, leaving ¼″ seam allowances and a 2″ opening at the top for turning. Turn to right side. Stuff firmly with fiberfill; turn edges at opening ¼″ to inside and slip-stitch closed except for ¼″ at center. Repeat to make three more strawberries.

4. Stems. Cut four ¾″ squares of felt and roll each up tightly to form a stem, stitching down side edge to close. Insert ⅛″ at end of each stem into top of a strawberry, and stitch opening closed, catching stem. Cut ¼″-long slit in center of each felt top. Slip a top over each stem and fold around berry. Tack in place by running needle with green thread back and forth through berry and top several times.

5. Rings. From green dotted fabric, cut four 2¾″ × 6½″ pieces. Fold each piece in half lengthwise, right sides together, and stitch lengthwise edges together, leaving ¼″ seam allowances. Turn inside out and stuff firmly with fiberfill, using eraser end of pencil to push it in. Turn short edges ¼″ to inside and slip-stitch together to form rings. Tack a ring at seam to center back of each strawberry.

Strawberry Pot holders and Coasters.

SIZES: Pot holder, 8½″ long; coaster, 4½″ long

MATERIALS

For two pot holders: ⅜ yard 36″-wide white-dot-on-red cotton fabric; large scrap solid green cotton fabric. Polyester batting. Red and green sewing thread.

For four coasters: ¼ yard each 36″-wide white-dot-on-green and white-dot-on-red cotton fabric. A 12″ square terry cloth. Red and green sewing thread.

NOTE: Directions are for pot holders; changes for coasters are in parentheses.

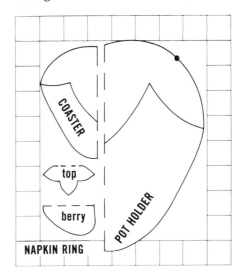

1. Making patterns. Using pencil and ruler, draw lines across strawberry pattern connecting grid lines. Enlarge pattern by copying design on paper ruled in 1″ squares. Make whole pattern by flopping and duplicating half pattern, indicated by dash lines.

2. Marking and cutting fabric. Using dressmaker's carbon and dry ball-point pen, transfer the following pieces for each pot holder (coaster) to right side of fabric: two strawberry tops to white-dot-on-green fabric, two whole strawberries to white-dot-on-red fabric. Cut out each piece along marked lines.

Place each strawberry top on whole berry piece, right sides up and top edges aligned;

baste in place. Using green thread and
$\frac{1}{16}$"-wide zigzag stitches, stitch top in place
along bottom edge. Using whole berry pattern,
cut batting (terry cloth) piece. With wrong
sides together and edges aligned, place
strawberry pieces together with batting (terry)
between them; baste.

3. The binding. From dotted red fabric, cut
$\frac{3}{4}$"-wide, $14\frac{1}{4}$"-long ($8\frac{1}{4}$"-long) strip for each
pot holder (coaster). From green (green-
dotted) fabric, cut $\frac{3}{4}$"-wide, $12\frac{1}{4}$"-long ($7\frac{1}{4}$"-
long) strip for each pot holder (coaster). Fold
and press raw edges $\frac{1}{8}$" to wrong side on all
strips. Press strips in half lengthwise, wrong
sides together. Use strip to bind raw edges of
each strawberry, stitching close to fold
through all thicknesses.

4. Hanging loop. To make each hanging
loop, cut $\frac{3}{4}$" x 5" ($\frac{3}{4}$" × 3") piece from green
(white-dot-on-green) fabric; double fold
lengthwise and press. Press ends $\frac{1}{8}$" to one
side, fold into a loop, and stitch the strip to
top of each berry as shown, with raw edges
inside.

Strawberry Jar Covers

SIZE: $2\frac{1}{2}$" in diameter

EQUIPMENT: Compass

MATERIALS: Scraps of green-dot-on-white,
white-dot-on-green, white-dot-on-red, and
solid green cotton fabrics. Sewing thread to
match fabrics. Baby green rickrack. One yard
$\frac{1}{4}$"-wide red satin ribbon. Polyester fiberfill.

1. Making patterns. Using pencil and
ruler, draw lines across strawberry appliqué
patterns, connecting grid lines; enlarge jar
cover pattern by copying design on paper
ruled in 1" squares. Using compass, make
pattern for 9"-diameter circle; cut out.

2. Marking and cutting the fabric. Use
circle pattern to cut two circles from green-
dot-on-white fabric for jar covers. Using
dressmaker's carbon and dry ball-point pen,
transfer appliqué pattern to center right side
of each cover piece.

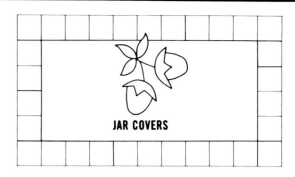

JAR COVERS

3. The appliqué. Referring to *How to
Appliqué* section at back of book, cut out and
prepare the following pieces for each cover,
as directed for machine appliqué: two berries
from red-dotted fabric, two berry tops from
green, and three leaves from white-dot-on-
green fabric.

Using closely spaced $\frac{1}{16}$"-wide zigzag
stitches, appliqué pieces to cover as directed,
and embroider fine stem lines (see pattern).
Turn edges of covers $\frac{1}{4}$" to wrong side and
stitch $\frac{1}{8}$" in from edge all around; press.

4. Finishing the jar covers. Cut a piece
of green rickrack to fit along edge of each
cover and topstitch on right side, overlapping
ends $\frac{1}{4}$". Place a ball of fiberfill on each jar
lid, then place a cover, right side up and
centered, on top. Cut ribbon in two; use half
to tie bow around base of each jar lid as
shown to hold cover in place.

Strawberry Biscuit Caddy

SIZE: Fits 8"-diameter basket

EQUIPMENT: Compass. Cardboard.

MATERIALS: Cotton fabrics: $\frac{3}{8}$" yard 36"-
wide white-dot-on-red; 2" × 40" green-dot-on-
white bias piece. Red and white sewing
threads. 8"-diameter white wicker basket.

1. Making pattern and cutting fabric.
Using compass, mark pattern for $12\frac{1}{2}$"-
diameter circle on cardboard; cut out. Use
pattern to cut two circles from red dotted
fabric. Cut white dotted fabric in half
lengthwise to make two 1"-wide strips. Fold
one short edge of each strip $\frac{1}{8}$" to wrong side,
then double-fold strip in half lengthwise,
wrong side in; press.

2. Assembling biscuit caddy. Enclose edge of each circle with a strip, overlapping ends; topstitch in place with white thread.

On right side of one circle, mark two lines crossing in center and dividing circle into quarters. Place circles wrong sides together with edges even. Using red thread, stitch along lines. Mark a point 1½" on either side of each stitched line at edge of circle. Stitch a line from this point to within 1½" of intersection, to make eight small segments. On top circle, pick up each of the four large segments and join in center; tack together for pockets. Place in basket.

Strawberry Toaster Cover

SIZE: Fits two-slice toaster

MATERIALS: Cotton fabrics: ½ yard 45"-wide green-dot-on-white; scraps of white-dot-on-red and solid green. ½ yard 36"-wide muslin for lining. 3 yards ⅜"-wide green double-fold bias tape. Polyester quilt batting. Sewing thread to match fabrics.

1. Making the patterns and marking and cutting the fabric. Using pencil and ruler, draw lines across strawberry appliqué and toaster cover patterns; complete half-pattern, indicated by dash line. Enlarge patterns by copying design on paper ruled in 1" squares; trace appliqué pattern. Use pattern for toaster cover to cut two pieces each from green-dot-on-white fabric, batting, and muslin; add ⅜" seam allowance to curved edge only.

Center tracing over one dotted piece (front) and transfer design to fabric, using dressmaker's carbon and dry ball-point pen.

2. The appliqué. Read *How to Appliqué* section at back of book. Using appliqué pattern, cut out the following pieces, as directed for machine appliqué: three strawberries from white-dot-on-red fabric, three berry tops and two leaves from green. Appliqué pieces as directed, setting machine for 1/16"-wide zigzag stitches; also embroider fine lines (see pattern).

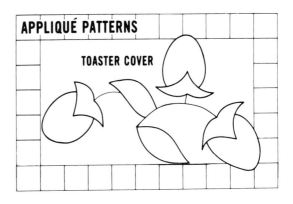

APPLIQUÉ PATTERNS

TOASTER COVER

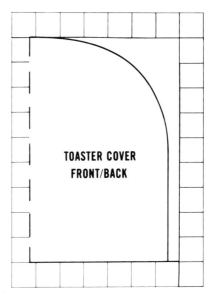

TOASTER COVER FRONT/BACK

3. Assembling the toaster cover. Separate muslin, batting, and fabric pieces into two sets for front and back of toaster cover. Stack each set with edges even, so that muslin is on bottom and fabric is right side up and on top, with batting between. Machine-baste ¼" in from edges all around.

To make cover gusset, cut 7" × 26½" strip each from muslin, batting, and green-dot-on-white fabric. Stack and baste pieces together as for cover front and back. With muslin sides together and edges even, pin curved edges of front and back pieces to long edges of gusset; stitch leaving ⅜" seam allowances.

Cut pieces of bias tape to fit and pin along curved edges of gusset, enclosing seam. Using matching thread, topstitch close to fold through all thicknesses. Cut bias tape to fit bottom edge plus 1" and finish bottom in same manner; fold ends under ¼" and overlap before stitching.

Pop Art Appliance Covers

Dress up your blender, mixer, can opener, and toaster with a soft-sculpture cover in bright, cheerful colors.

SIZES: Soup cover, 13″ × 9½″. Bread cover, 9″ × 12″. Flour cover, 14″ × 18″, Milk cover, 8″ × 17″.

EQUIPMENT: Colored pencil. Thin, stiff cardboard. Tailor's chalk. Compass.

MATERIALS: 45″-wide soft cotton or cotton-blend fabrics. **Soup:** ¼ yard each red and yellow; ⅝ yard gray. **Milk:** 1 yard white, ¼ yard each blue and green. **Flour:** ¾ yard yellow; 1 yard orange. **Bread:** ¾ yard white, ⅛ yard red. Batting. Thread to match all fabrics.

General Directions

1. Making patterns and marking and cutting fabric. Using a sharp colored pencil, draw lines connecting grid lines across pattern for letter appliqués. Enlarge pattern by drawing designs on paper ruled in 1″ squares. Following appliqué directions in *How to Appliqué* section and individual directions following, cut pieces from fabric and batting; dimensions given include seam allowances.

2. The machine appliqué. Machine-appliqué letters and other pieces as directed under individual projects to one (outer) main piece, using sewing thread to match appliqués. Baste batting to wrong side of outer piece. Place outer and inner pieces right sides together, and stitch around edges leaving ½″ seam allowances and opening for turning where necessary. Grade seams, trimming batting close to stitching. Turn piece to right side through opening; slip-stitch opening closed.

3. Finishing. Using thread to match background, topstitch through all layers around letters and where directed, working from center of piece out to edges. Assemble cover as directed; slip-stitch butted edges together.

Toaster Cover

1. Marking and cutting fabric. Cut two pieces from white fabric and one piece from batting, each 19″ × 23″. Cut two sets of "BREAD" letters from red fabric.

2. The appliqué. Appliqué one set of letters on right side of one white fabric piece (outer piece), placing letters 3½″ above long edge nearest you and centering them between sides. Turn piece around so that opposite long edge is nearest you, and appliqué second set of letters in same manner.

3. Assembling and finishing cover. Baste batting to wrong side of outer piece. Stitch white pieces right sides together, around edges, leaving opening for turning. Trim seam allowances, turn, close opening. Topstitch around letters and all around edges. Fold piece in half crosswise, appliquéd side inward and bottom edges aligned; slip-stitch the ends closed. Turn to right side. Fold in half, with the two side seams centered. Fold down top of upper side seam 3″, forming a triangle; slip-stitch lower edges of triangle in place. Repeat for other side of cover.

Can opener Cover

1. Marking and cutting fabric. From gray fabric, cut 27¾″ × 11¾″ piece; using compass, cut two round 9″-diameter pieces. From red and yellow fabric, cut one 5½″ × 27¾″ piece and one set of "SOUP" letters from each. From batting, cut 10¾″ × 27″ piece and round 8″-diameter piece.

2. Assembling label. To make can label, place red and yellow pieces right sides together, and stitch on one long edge. Trim seam allowances; press open. Appliqué "SOUP" letters to right side of each section, parallel to and 1″ from seam and centered between sides; place red on yellow and yellow on red and face all letters in same direction. Turn edges of label under ½″ all around; press.

3. Finishing side of can. To finish side of can, place rectangular gray piece flat, wrong side up. Center rectangular batting over gray piece; turn fabric edges over batting, short sides first, then top and bottom, mitering corners; baste in place.

4. Joining top and side. Pin can label right side up over batting and fabric edges, centering so there is a ⅜″ gray margin at top and bottom and a ⅛″ margin at sides.

Topstitch along seam joining red and yellow section, around letters and around edges of label. Slip-stitch side edges right sides together to form a tube.

5. Making top and finishing cover. To make top of can, baste batting to wrong side of a gray circle. Stitch gray pieces right sides together, leaving opening. Trim seam allowances, turn, close opening. With compass, mark 3½"- and 6½"-diameter circles in center of top. Topstitch along lines. Slip-stitch top to side, right sides together, around upper edge. Turn cover to right side.

Mixer Cover

1. Marking and cutting fabric. From yellow fabric, cut two 19½" × 22" pieces and two sets of "FLOUR" letters. From orange fabric, cut two 19½" × 22" pieces, two 8" × 12½" pieces, and four 1½" × 22" strips. Cut two 19½" × 22" batting pieces. Fold each 8" × 12½" orange piece in half twice lengthwise and round off unfolded corner, for long oval.

2. The appliqué. Place each yellow (outer) piece so that longest edges are at top and bottom. Appliqué the following to each: an orange strip 1½" from bottom edge and an orange strip 3½" from top edge; an orange oval centered lengthwise between the strips; the letters FLOUR centered lengthwise on the oval.

3. Assembling and finishing the cover. Baste batting to yellow pieces. Sew yellow pieces right sides together along one side. Sew orange pieces together in same manner. Place orange and yellow pieces right sides together, and stitch together at top and bottom, leaving ½" free at each end. Trim seam allowances. Turn to right side.

Topstitch around letters, ovals, and strips, and at top and bottom edges, leaving ends free as before. Turn piece to orange side.

Pin side edges of orange piece back ½"; stitch side edges of yellow piece together. Trim. Unpin orange edges, fold under, and slip-stitch together. Slip-stitch top edges together. Placing piece flat, fold in top corners 3" toward center; slip-stitch in place along top edge. Turn cover to right side.

Each square = 1"

Blender Cover

1. Marking and cutting fabric. From white fabric, cut 12½" × 31" piece and 18½" × 31" piece. From blue fabric, cut 6" × 31" piece. From green fabric, cut 2" × 31" piece and six sets of "MILK" letters. Cut 18½" × 31" batting piece.

2. Assembling outer piece. To assemble outer piece, sew smaller white piece to blue piece along lengthwise edges, then green piece to other long edge of blue piece. Outer piece should measure 18½" × 31", same as larger white (inner) piece.

3. Marking outer piece for appliqué. Lay outer piece flat, right side up and with long edges at top and bottom. Using ruler and tailor's chalk, lightly mark ½" seam allowances at sides, then mark off the 30" area between seam lines into four 7½"-wide sections (see vertical dash lines on diagram). Mark another line 1" above the seam joining white and blue piece, as shown. Mark a triangle above this line in second and fourth marked sections. Mark six A lines as shown.

4. The appliqué. Appliqué the words "MILK" to each A line with bottom of letters resting on line. Baste batting to wrong side of outer piece. Place inner and outer pieces with right sides together; stitch along top and bottom edges, leaving ½″ free at each end. Trim seam allowances and turn piece to right side.

5. Finishing cover. Topstitch along marked (dash) lines, around letters, and along top and bottom edges, leaving ends free as before. Fold piece along horizontal topstitching on blue sections and stitch through all layers close to fold, making a ridge; unfold.

Turn piece to inner side. Pin side edges of inner piece back ½″; stitch side edges of outer piece together. Trim. Unpin inner edges, fold under, and slip-stitch together. Slip-stitch top edges of cover together. Placing piece flat, fold in top corners until they meet at center; slip-stitch in place along top edge. Turn cover to right side. At top, slip-stitch green side edges together.

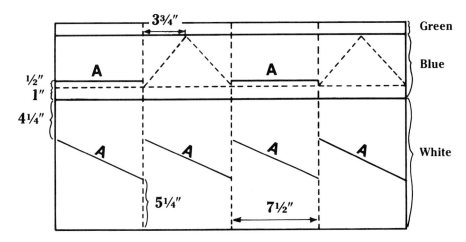

Diagram for Blender Cover

A Plenitude of
Patchwork Pot Holders

Any one of these six different pot holders would make a great addition to any kitchen, and all of the designs lend themselves equally well to larger projects, such as an heirloom quilt.

MATERIALS: Preshrunk pieces of tightly woven cotton fabric in solid colors and small prints as shown or as desired. White and matching sewing thread. Outing flannel for padding. 1"-diameter white plastic ring for each.

1. Making the patterns and marking and cutting the fabric.
Enlarge patterns by copying designs on paper ruled in 1" squares; complete quarter-patterns indicated by long dash lines. The fine dash lines indicate quilting lines. Make a separate cardboard pattern for each part of design. Cut patches according to directions for *How to Quilt* at back of book, marking on wrong side of fabric and adding ¼" seam allowance all around each piece.

2. Assembling pot holder.
Following patterns, sew all the pieces together to complete pot holder tops. For back, cut one complete pot holder shape of matching or contrasting solid-color fabric, adding ¼" all around for seam allowance.

For each pot holder, cut two thicknesses of flannel the shape of pot holder but ⅜" smaller all around. Baste both layers of flannel to top to hold in place. Place the top and back right sides together, sew together along edges, leaving ¼" seam allowances and an opening large enough for turning pot holder to right side. Turn to right side; turn edges of opening in ¼"; sew closed.

Each pot holder is quilted through all thicknesses with white sewing thread. Quilt along all fine dash lines (see pattern) and along some seams. Remove basting stitches. Sew ring to back near edge of pot holder.

Pattern A: Cut 5¼" white square for piece 1; cut pieces 2 of white; cut piece 3 of orange; cut pieces 4 of five different printed fabrics; cut pieces 5 of gold color. Sew the pieces of the fan shape together; pin in place on piece 1; turn under edges of points and sew in place. Sew pieces 2 in place. Cut ¾"-wide bias strips of solid-colored fabric and sew together leaving ¼" seam allowances to make one strip long enough to fit all around pot holder. Sew one edge of strip all around pot holder top, right sides together and leaving ⅛" seam allowances. Turn binding to back. Turn raw

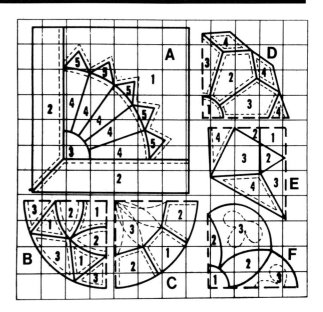

edge under ⅛" and slip-stitch to fabric, mitering corners.

Pattern B: Cut pieces 1 of orange; cut pieces 2 of yellow; cut pieces 3 of white. For ruffled edge, cut a strip about 45" long and 1½" wide of orange on the bias. Sew ends right sides together, leaving ¼" seam allowances. Turn to right side. Fold in half lengthwise; press. Gather raw edge to fit circumference of pot holder. Before sewing top and back together, baste ruffle around top with right sides together and raw edges aligned. When sewing top and back together, make sure ruffle is on inside.

Pattern C: Cut pieces 1 of red; cut pieces 2 of red-and-white checked gingham; cut piece 3 of white. Sew together and quilt by machine, using red thread for center design, white for other quilting. Make ruffled edge as for Pattern B.

Pattern D: Cut piece 1 of bright pink; cut pieces 2 of dark green; cut pieces 3 of pink print; cut pieces 4 of white.

Pattern E: Cut piece 1 of blue; cut pieces 2 of orange; cut pieces 3 of blue-yellow print; cut pieces 4 of yellow.

Pattern F: Cut piece 1 of orange; cut pieces 2 of yellow; cut pieces 3 of aqua. Quilt through all thicknesses only along seams. Stitch along short dash lines through top fabric only and draw thread up tightly for puckered effect.

Cheerful Kitchen Witch

Invite luck into your kitchen with the presence
of this jovial kitchen witch.

SIZE: 16″ × 12″

EQUIPMENT: Knitting needle.

MATERIALS: ½ yard 36″-wide unbleached muslin. Cotton fabrics: Small amounts orange, white-on-brown dotted, tan calico; brown. White, orange, and brown sewing thread. Ten assorted 12″-30″ wheat and grass stalks. Orange pearl cotton #5. 1″-diameter plastic ring. Fiberfill.

1. Making patterns and marking and cutting fabric.
Using pencil and ruler, draw lines across patterns, connecting grid lines. Enlarge patterns by copying on paper ruled in

KITCHEN WITCH

Each square = 1″

1″ squares. Heavy lines indicate appliqués, fine lines embroidery. Transfer outline of witch to right side of two pieces of muslin. Referring to photograph, transfer individual appliqué designs to right side of other fabrics. Cut out all pieces ¼″ beyond marked lines for seam allowances.

2. The appliqué and embroidery.
Following directions in *How to Appliqué* section at back of book and using orange thread, machine-appliqué apron to right side of dress front as shown, using zigzag stitch set at ¹⁄₁₆″. Still using orange thread, appliqué dress and remaining pieces to right side of one muslin piece (front), following pattern for placement and changing zigzag stitch to ⅛″; stitch witch's profile along marked lines.

Changing back to ¹⁄₁₆″-wide stitches, but still using orange thread, machine-embroider hands, arms, and apron. Use finest zigzag for mouth. Thread machine with brown to satin-stitch eye.

3. Assembling and finishing witch.
Pin muslin pieces right sides together and edges even; stitch with white thread, leaving ¼″ seam allowances and a 4″ opening at bottom. Clip into seam allowances at curves and across corners; turn to right side and poke out corners with knitting needle.

Stuff firmly with fiberfill. Turn raw edges ¼″ to inside; slip-stitch opening closed. Wrap orange pearl cotton around wheat stalks about 3″ from cut ends. Slip-stitch stalks to back of witch at arms and skirt, as shown in photograph. Slip-stitch plastic ring behind neck, for hanging.

Quilted, Leafy Place Mat Set

Four different trees inspired these leaf-shaped place mats and the seeds that decorate the coordinated napkins. The place mats are machine-quilted and the napkins are machine-appliquéd. Of course, if you prefer one shape to the others, you can simply make as many duplicates as you want.

SIZE: Place mats vary from about 13″ wide by 14″ high, excluding leaf tips; napkins are 17″ square.

MATERIALS: ⅝ yard 45″-wide cotton calico in colors desired for each placemat; 18″ solid-color cotton square for each napkin, to coordinate with place mat; contrasting calico scraps for appliqués. Fiberfill batting for padding place mats. Matching and contrasting sewing thread.

Place Mats

1. Making patterns and marking and cutting fabric. Enlarge patterns for leaves and motifs by copying designs on paper ruled in 1″ squares. Heavy lines indicate seam lines. Fine lines indicate zigzag stitching lines.

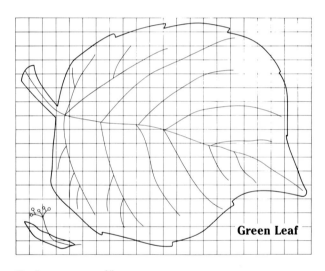

Each square = 1″

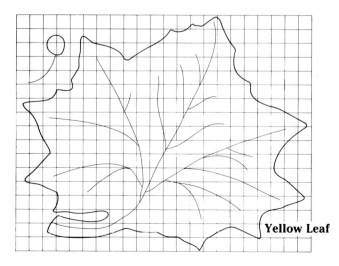

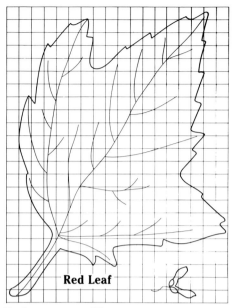

Red Leaf

Each square = 1″

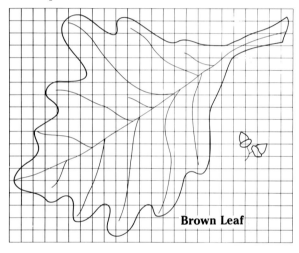

Brown Leaf

Pin patterns on doubled fabric; cut out, adding ¼″ all around for seam allowance. Using dry ball-point pen and carbon paper, transfer leaf vein lines to right side of one fabric piece. Using leaf pattern, cut a piece of fiberfill ⅛″ smaller all around.

2. Assembling placemat. Place fiberfill layer on wrong side of unmarked calico leaf; baste in place.

Stitch the two leaf pieces for place mat, right sides together, leaving ¼″ seam allowances and stem, plus 2″ on either side of stem, open for turning. Clip into seam allowances; turn leaf to right side. Push out points and curves of leaf with scissors' point. Turn in seam allowances around opening and slip-stitch closed. Press edges lightly.

3. Machine quilting. On marked side of leaf, pin all thicknesses together in unmarked areas, smoothing out leaf. With close zigzag stitches and contrasting thread, stitch along marked lines through all thicknesses; use a slightly wider zigzag stitch for center vein.

Napkins

1. Stitching hem. On square piece, turn ½″ on all edges to wrong side, mitering corners; press. Turn raw edges of hem under ⅛″; press. Using medium-width zigzag stitches and matching thread, stitch hem along turned edge.

2. The appliqué. Trace enlarged motif for napkin appliqué. Referring to *How to Appliqué* section and using carbon paper and dry ball-point pen, transfer motifs to desired fabrics (choose colors that will contrast with the napkin color). Cut appliqué pieces and pin near one corner of napkin; then mark stem for each, indicated by fine lines on patterns. Using close, narrow zigzag stitches and matching thread, appliqué pieces as directed; stitch along stem lines.

Reversible Calico and Gingham Place Mats

These handsome place mats do double duty with a different design on each side, and they can be made in a jiffy with the help of zigzag stitching. Make them to coordinate with your decor by simply choosing fabrics of different colors.

SIZES: Place mats, 12″ × 18″. Napkins, 15″ square.

MATERIALS: 44″-wide cotton or cotton-blend fabric: 1 yard ¼″ check green-and-white gingham; 1 yard green-yellow-and-red calico. ¼ yard Pellon®. ⅔ yard 36″-wide heavyweight Pellon® interfacing. Sewing thread.

Place Mats

1. Cutting the fabric. Cut two 12½″ × 18½″ pieces each of gingham and of calico and two 12″ × 18″ pieces of heavyweight Pellon®. Center one piece of Pellon® on wrong side of each gingham piece; baste in place.

Cut two 1½″-wide × 12½″-long and two 1½″-wide × 18″-long calico strips. Repeat for gingham strips. Turn under raw lengthwise edges ¼″ to wrong side; press.

2. Assembling the place mat sides. To make the gingham sides, pin a 12½″-long calico strip 2″ in from one 12½″ edge; repeat on opposite side. Straight stitch close to each long edge of strips, then zigzag stitch over edge and stitching. Repeat on other two sides with the 18½″-long calico strips, completing one side of mat. Repeat for second mat.

Make the reverse sides of mats in same manner, using calico rectangles and gingham strips.

3. Joining front and back of mats. Pin the two mat pieces for each mat right sides together. Stitch all around, leaving ¼″ seam allowances and a 4″ opening on one long side. Turn mat to right side. Turn under seam allowances along opening and slip-stitch closed. Zigzag stitch all around edge of place mat.

Napkins

Cut two 16″ squares from both calico and gingham. Fold under ¼″ twice around edges of each and topstitch ⅛″ in from fold all around napkin.

Cottage and Tabby Cat Tea Cozies with a Dresden Plate Mat

Quilted tea cozies help hold the comforting warmth in a pot of tea, and a large patchwork plate mat not only brightens the table but protects it from heat and spills.

Cottage Tea Cozy

EQUIPMENT: Quilting needles. Tailor's chalk.

MATERIALS: Closely woven cotton fabric: ¾ yard 36″-wide yellow; 6″ × 14″ piece of gray; scraps of red, green, white, and calico for appliqués. ⅜ yard soft fabric for interlining. Matching sewing thread. Dacron batting. DMC pearl cotton, size 5: one ball each of black #310, green #907, yellow #973, and blue #798. Small amounts of embroidery floss: gold, red, white, and blue.

1. Making the pattern and marking and cutting the house pieces. Enlarge house pattern by copying design on paper ruled in 1″ squares; add 1″ to bottom of pattern for hem. Dash lines indicate quilting lines.

Using dressmaker's carbon and tracing wheel, mark outline only of house four times on wrong side of yellow fabric, leaving at least ½" between pieces. Cut out each of the house pieces, adding ¼" around the edges for seam allowances.

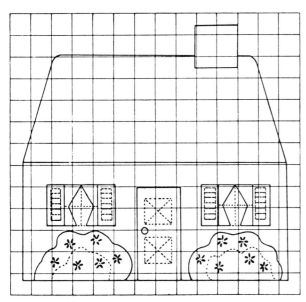

Cottage Tea Cozy   **Each square = 1"**

2. The appliqué and embroidery.

Referring to the *How to Appliqué* section at back of book, mark position of appliqués on right side of one house section. Do not cut out. Cut out appliqués for roof, door, shutters, curtains, and bushes in colors shown, adding ¼" around all edges to turn under. Slip-stitch appliqués in place on marked house piece.

Embroider flowers in embroidery floss with lazy daisy stitch petals and French knot centers; work doorknob in satin stitch. (See *Embroidery Stitches.*)

3. Quilting.
Mark the horizontal quilting lines on house and roof ½" apart, using ruler and tailor's chalk. Mark vertical shingle lines on roof 1" apart, alternating placement on every other row as shown in photograph. Transfer quilting lines from pattern to shutters, windows, door, and bushes, using dressmaker's carbon and tracing wheel. Using house pattern, cut a batting and an interlining section. Pin and baste all together, with right sides of yellow fabric facing.

Quilt roof shingles with blue pearl cotton; house siding with yellow; shutters with green;

around and inside bushes with green; window panes, outlines of door and paneling with black. Stitch quilted house and one unquilted house right sides together on all sides except bottom. Leave wrong side out.

4. The lining. Cut house shape from interlining fabric and from batting, adding ¼" seam allowances; add 1" hem on bottom of interlining. Mark 2" grid on interlining piece, using ruler and tailor's chalk. Pin and baste interlining piece to wrong side of a yellow house piece, with batting in between. Machine-stitch along grid lines.

Stitch quilted interlining to third yellow house piece along three sides, with right sides of yellow fabric together; leave wrong side out.

5. Assembling the cozy. Assemble lining and outer piece as for Tabby Tea Cozy.

6. The chimney. Mark pattern on right side of red fabric (front chimney); mark chimney shape again directly above to double pattern (back chimney). With ruler and tailor's chalk, mark quilting lines on front chimney only; four horizontal lines ½" apart; two vertical lines in first and third rows, one vertical line in second and fourth row. Cut out batting and interlining in double chimney shaped pattern. Pin and baste batting and interlining beneath red fabric; quilt on marked lines with yellow pearl cotton. Mark parallel lines 1" beyond both sides of chimney for added width. Cut out entire red piece, adding ¼" all around for seam allowance. Fold in half lengthwise, right sides together. Stitch lengthwise seam. Turn right side out and press so that seam is in center of back. Finish both ends by turning in raw edges and slip-stitching closed. Fold in half crosswise with ends of chimney overlapping front and back of roof; slip-stitch in place.

Tabby Tea Cozy

EQUIPMENT: Quilting needles.

MATERIALS: Lightweight cotton fabric such as broadcloth: ⅔ yard 36"-wide beige; scraps of royal blue. ⅜ yard soft fabric such as Poly-SiBonne, for interlining. Dacron batting. DMC pearl cotton, size 5: one ball each light orange #741, yellow #973, navy #336, maroon #815, gold #783. Beige sewing thread.

1. Making the patterns. Enlarge patterns for cat body and separate head by copying design on paper ruled in 1″ squares; complete half-pattern details on head, indicated by dash lines, by flopping pattern along line and tracing it.

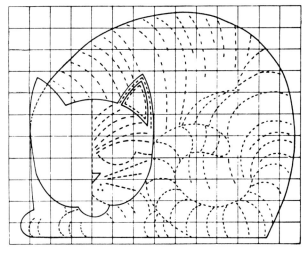

Tabby Tea Cozy   Each square = 1″

2. Marking and appliquéing front. Transfer patterns onto beige fabric, marking on right side of fabric with dressmaker's carbon and tracing wheel, leaving at least 1″ between the two patterns and 1″ along bottom of cat body for hem; do not cut out. Transfer dash line quilting design. Cut two inner ears of blue fabric allowing ¼″ all around to turn under; slip-stitch appliqués to head.

3. Quilting front. Pin and baste marked beige fabric right side out to interlining, with batting between them. Quilt along dash lines with pearl cotton, making stitches about ⅛″-¼″ long. Make tiger stripe lines yellow and orange, referring to photograph; outline ears in orange; make whiskers, mouth, paws, outline of tail and leg, and inside of ears maroon; make eyes navy. Embroider yellow French knots under nose; embroider nose with gold satin stitches. (See *Embroidery Stitches.*)

Cut out the cat head and body, adding ¼″ all around for seam allowance, plus 1″ hem at bottom of body.

4. Completing outside of cat. Cut one more head piece and one more body from beige fabric, marking pattern on wrong side of fabric and adding ¼″ seam allowance all around, plus 1″ hem at bottom of body. Stitch quilted and unquilted head pieces right sides together, leaving 2″ opening for turning. Turn head right side out; slip-stitch closed.

Sew quilted cat body and unquilted body right sides together along curve, leaving bottom open and piece wrong side out.

5. The lining. Cut one cat body from interlining fabric and one from batting, and two from beige fabric, adding ¼″ seam allowances and 1″ hem on the bottoms.

Mark 2″ grid on the interlining piece, using ruler and tailor's chalk. Pin and baste interlining piece and a beige body piece wrong sides together, with batting in between. Machine-stitch along grid lines. Stitch quilted interlining to another cat body section along curved edge, with right sides of beige fabric together; leave wrong side out.

6. Assembling cozy. Place lining and outer piece together so that unquilted side of outer piece faces quilted side of lining; pin and baste along curved edge, leaving last 2″ free at beginning and end of curve; stitch. Turn outer piece over lining, so that wrong sides of both pieces are on the inside of tea cozy. Turn up both lining and outer piece separately for 1″ at bottom, so that hems are hidden inside tea cozy; slip-stitch closed along bottom edge. Position cat's head on body and slip-stitch in place.

Dresden Plate Mat

SIZE: 14¾″ diameter.

EQUIPMENT: Compass. Thin, stiff cardboard.

MATERIALS: ¼ yard of 36″-wide cotton print in each of four different background colors, such as white, red, yellow, and blue. ½ yard 36″-wide tightly woven lightweight fabric for lining and interlining. One 14½" circle Pellon® fleece. 2 yards rickrack. Sewing thread to match fabrics.

1. Cutting the patches. Read *How to Quilt* section at back of book. On tracing paper, complete half-pattern indicated by dash line. Cut complete pattern out of cardboard.

Mark 4 patches ½" apart on each fabric print as follows. Place cardboard pattern on wrong side of printed fabric; with pencil, trace around pattern outline. Cut out patch, adding ¼" seam allowances beyond marked outline at side edges only. The marked lines on fabric will be seam lines.

2. Patching the top. Cut out 15" circle from interlining fabric; cut 5" circle from center. Sew patches to interlining, alternating the four colors. Place first patch right side up on interlining with edges even. Pin and sew along seam line of one long side. Place second patch on top of first patch, right sides together, aligning stitched side seam line and seam line of second patch. Stitch through all thicknesses along side seam line. Flop second patch over to right side; press.

With right sides facing, place next patch on top of previous patch, aligning unstitched side seam lines. Stitch through all thicknesses along matching seam line. Flop this patch over to right side; press. Repeat from * to * until all patches are used.

At end, cut into interlining along raw edge of first patch. Pull side edges of first and last patches out through cut in interlining with right sides facing; sew these edges together. Insert back through opening. Stitch all around ¼" in from outer edges to mark seam line.

3. Finishing the plate mat. Cut a 15" circle from lining fabric. Center and baste Pellon® circle to lining. Baste rickrack around outside edge of right side of patched top, with center of rickrack on seam line.

Baste patched top to lining, right sides together. Stitch together all around outer edge, leaving ¼" seam allowances. Turn right

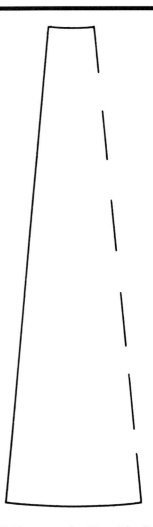

Actual-size Half-pattern for Plate Mat Patch

side out through center opening; press. To keep work flat, topstitch around center opening ⅜" in from raw edges through all thicknesses.

Cut 6¼" circle from one remaining piece of print fabric; stitch ⅜" from outer edge to mark seam line. Center rickrack over seam line and stitch. Turn edge of circle under ⅜" all around, leaving only tips of rickrack exposed; press. Baste circle over opening of patched top. Topstitch over rickrack, as close to edge of circle as possible, stitching through all layers. To quilt, stitch on right side along seam lines between patches. Stitch through all layers.

P A R T II

PERSONAL AND DECORATIVE ACCESSORIES

Whether you are looking for a gift idea or want to create something for yourself or your home, you are sure to find something to please you in this section. Choose a pretty and personal project like a patchwork billfold or a fabric-covered picture frame. Or create a distinctive pillow, wall-hanging, or quilted cachepot to accent a room, choosing from the wide variety of designs presented.

Dressing Up a Desk: Fabric-covered Folders, Frames, Boxes, and Bookends

Any desk top will be enhanced by the addition of a well-chosen fabric-covered accessory, such as one of the eight shown here. Create the look you want by the design of the fabric you select—"all business," "country," "feminine" . . . you decide.

EQUIPMENT: Mat knife. Two push-pins and string for oval mirror frame.

MATERIALS: "Scotch" Spra-Ment Spray adhesive. "Scotch" Super Strength Adhesive for trims, oval or rectangular mirror, and folding frame. "Scotchgard" fabric protector. Tightly woven fabrics, amounts determined by object to be covered. See individual directions for additional materials.

General Directions

Determine the size and shape of fabric needed to cover item, following specifications given in individual directions and diagrams. On the diagrams, solid lines indicate cutting lines, dash lines indicate folding lines. Mark size and shape on paper to use as pattern, cut out pattern, then cut out fabric piece, following individual directions.

If desired, two color-coordinated fabrics may be combined to cover a single item, as shown in photograph.

To adhere fabric, spray item to be covered on wrong side with Spra-Ment adhesive, following directions on can. Wait a few moments for surface to get tacky, then press fabric to item and smooth with fingers. Use Super Strength adhesive in tube for gluing trims where indicated. To keep fabrics from getting soiled, spray them with "Scotchgard" after project has been completed.

Open Folders

For each side of folder, cut a piece of fabric the length of the folder and the height of the folder plus 5⅜". Glue fabric piece to each side of folder, folding over to inside 5" at top and ⅜" at bottom. Trim away excess fabric flush with curved corners of folder.

To trim large folder, cut two pieces of ribbon ¾" longer than length of folder. Using Super Strength adhesive, glue ribbon along bottom edges of folder, folding ends into accordion folds at sides. For ties, cut two more ribbons, each 15" long. With scissors, pierce hole on front and back of folder, ½" from center top edges. Slip one end of each ribbon through a hole and knot end on inside.

Folder With Flap

Carefully remove elastic or string tie from folder. For front of folder (not flap), cut piece of fabric the length of folder and the height plus 2". Glue fabric to front, folding 2" margin over top to inside. Cut back and flap fabric in one piece, following Diagram A, adding 1" to underside of flap at each side. Glue back in place, then top of flap, sides of flap, and underside of flap.

Replace elastic or string tie.

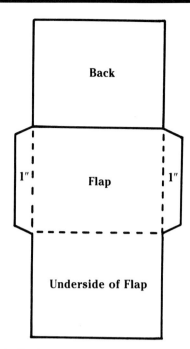

Diagram A: Back and flap pattern for folder with flap

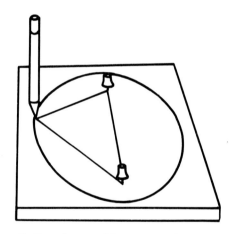

Diagram B: Drawing oval frame opening

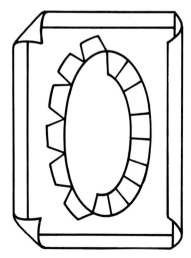

Diagram C: Gluing fabric to oval frame

Small Folding Picture Frame

For mat, cut 9½″ × 7″ piece of cardboard. Cut out a 6½″ × 4½″ area from center. Cut fabric the length and width of mat, adding 1″ margins all around. Glue front of mat, centered to wrong side of fabric. With mat knife, cut out center of fabric 1″ smaller than inner cardboard edges. Slit fabric diagonally to inner corners of mat. Glue excess fabric to back, around both inner and outer edges.

For frame cover, cut 10″ × 14½″ piece of sturdy cardboard. Lightly score cross-wise along but not through center. Cut two pieces of fabric: one the width and length of cardboard cover and one the width and length plus 1″ all around. Center outside of cardboard cover on wrong side of larger fabric piece; glue. Fold over and glue 1″ margins to inside. Glue other piece of fabric to inside.

Using Super Strength adhesive, glue mat to one half of inside cover ¼″ from three edges, leaving left side unglued to insert photograph.

Oval Mirror Frame

Draw oval opening in center of 12″ × 16″ mat as follows. Tie ends of a piece of string together to form an 18¾″ continuous loop. Insert two pushpins 7⅞″ apart into lengthwise center of rectangular board at least 12″ long and 9″ wide (see Diagram B). Place string loop around the two push-pins. Place point of pencil inside loop. Hold string taut as you move pencil around mat board to make an oval about 8″ × 10½″ (see Diagram B).

Cut out oval with mat knife. Cut fabric and thin layer of batting, each 13½″ × 17½″. Glue batting to wrong side of fabric. Center and glue frame to batting. Do not glue flaps.

Cut fabric from center of frame to within 1″ of oval edge. Clip 1″ fabric margin to edge of cardboard and glue margin to back (Diagram C). With Super Strength adhesive, glue mirror to back of frame. Fold fabric flaps over to back; miter corners and glue.

Cut 11″ × 15″ piece stiff cardboard; center and glue to mirror back with Super Strength adhesive. Following package directions, attach wall hook to cardboard back.

File Box

For this project a 10¼″ × 12½″ × 2¼″ open wooden box was used. To cover box, cut fabric pieces as follows: two 6″ × 14″, one 6″ × 12″, two 4″ × 12″, one 10″ × 12½″, and one 1″ × 12″. (**Note:** Adjust dimensions proportionately for box of different size.)

Glue 6″ × 14″ strips to long outer sides, bottom edges flush with box bottom and equal amount extending at each end; glue excess fabric around corners. Smooth fabric around corners. Smooth fabric over top to inside. Using mat knife, slit fabric to make inside corners fit neatly; glue. Glue 6″ × 12″ piece to outer back of box in same manner, folding margins under at corners to hide raw edges.

Trace front of box on paper, adding ¼″ to each side end. Using paper pattern, cut shape from the two 4″ × 12″ fabric strips. Glue to front inner and outer surfaces, folding under ¼″ margins.

Fold all edges of 1″ × 12″ strip under to fit front top edge, trimming if necessary; glue to box. Glue edges of large remaining piece under ¼″ and glue piece to inside of box. Glue felt on bottom of box.

Picture Frame

For this project, a 14″ × 16″ × 1″ wooden frame with a 7¾″ × 9¾″ opening was used. To cover frame, cut fabric pieces as follows: two 5″ × 15½″, two 5″ × 17½″ and two 2″ × 32½″. (**Note:** Adjust dimensions proportionately for frame of different size.)

Glue 5″ × 17½″ strips to long sides of frame, covering ¼″ of outer edges. At inside corners, slit fabric diagonally; pull fabric through frame opening, and glue raw edge to back.

Measure 8″ section in center of one long side of 5″ × 15½″ strip; mark with two straight pins. Glue strips to short sides of frame, with 8″ centers at inner edges; fold under fabric edges beyond 8″ sections for mitered corners. Pull 8″ raw edge through frame opening and glue to back.

Fold all raw edges of 2″ × 32½″ strip under ½″. Starting at one corner, glue strip around outside edge of frame. Cover remaining exposed edge with second strip, slightly overlapping first strip at ends.

Glue felt to back, leaving space around frame opening to slip picture inside.

Pencil Box

Cut fabric to fit around sides of box or tin can, adding ½″ on all edges. Glue fabric around box, folding margins to bottom and to top inside and overlapping side edges. Glue felt circles to inner and outer bottom. Glue felt to cover inside of box.

Bookends

Use plain metal bookends. Cut piece of cardboard to fit outside of each bookend; score cardboard so it bends at angle. Cut fabric pieces ½″ larger all around than cardboard pieces. Glue fabric to cardboard, folding over straight edges to back, then corners. With Super Strength adhesive, glue fabric-covered cardboard to bookends.

Cut-and-Fold Patchwork Accessories: Sachet, Box, Change Purse, Billfold, Key Ring, and Pincushion

Following the cut-and-fold technique used to make these intricate-looking accessories, the look of fine patchwork can be achieved in a fraction of the time it takes to do traditional piecing.

SIZES: Sachet, 4″ square. Box, 3″ × 3″ × 3″. Change purse, 4″ × 4⅛″. Billfold, 6¾″ × 3⅜″. Key ring, 1½″ square. Pincushion, 5″ square.

EQUIPMENT: 8 squares-to-the-inch graph paper. Thin, stiff cardboard. White craft glue. Knitting needle.

MATERIALS: Scraps of closely woven cotton fabric in three assorted prints (A, B, and C in diagrams) and one dotted (D) fabric; see photograph for colors. Sewing thread to match fabrics.

For sachet: 13″ piece ¾″-wide pre-ruffled cotton eyelet. Cotton balls for stuffing. Potpourri oil.

For box: 1⅜ yards ⅛″-diameter satin rattail cord to coordinate with fabrics. Cardboard. Batting.

For change purse: ¾″ × 4″ Velcro® strip.

For billfold: ¼ yard 18″-wide non-woven interfacing.

For key ring: 4″ length ⅛-wide satin ribbon to coordinate with fabrics.

For pincushion: 17″ length ¾″-wide white pre-ruffled cotton eyelet. Crushed potpourri.

General Directions

The "patchwork" blocks on all items are made by cutting and folding squares and rectangles.

1. Cutting fabric. Mark squares and rectangles on graph paper as directed below. Glue graph paper to cardboard, then cut out along marked lines to make templates. Mark pieces on fabric as directed, marking as many pieces as needed at one time: Place template on fabric with two parallel edges on straight of grain. Holding sharp, hard pencil at an outward angle, mark around template. Cut out pieces along marked lines.

2. Folding fabric. Following directions for individual projects, fold fabric pieces into squares, triangles, and strips; press and pin to keep folds in place: To form a folded square, place a fabric square face down on ironing board; bring top edge down to meet bottom, folding square in half horizontally; press; fold again in half vertically; press and pin. For folded triangle, press fabric square in half horizontally; then bring top corners of piece down to meet at center of bottom edge; press and pin. To form a folded strip, press fabric rectangle in half lengthwise, right side out; pin.

Sachet, Box, and Purse

1. Cutting and folding fabric. Make two templates, a 2″ square and a 2″ × 3½″ rectangle. Referring to photograph and diagram for color scheme, cut four squares from fabric A, six squares each from B and C, and four rectangles from D. Fold pieces as described in General Directions to form four

squares from A pieces, four squares and two triangles each from B's and C's, and four strips from D's. Cut 3½″ square of fabric for block backing. Use pencil to lightly mark horizontal and vertical center lines on right side of backing.

2. Assembling Block I design. Referring to diagram and working from center outward, assemble Block I for each project as follows. Pin two A squares and two B squares to backing, so that folded corners meet at center. Using double-threaded needle, tack centers and outer corners to backing.

Pin remaining A and B squares in place, overlapping center squares, so that inner corners are ¼″ from center of design and outer edges extend ¼″ beyond first squares: tack down corners as before.

Pin two D strips each to top and bottom of design, overlapping second squares ½″ and first squares ¼″ with folded edges; raw edges should be even with backing. Tack. Attach two D strips to each side of design in same manner.

Pin and tack C squares to corners of design, matching outer edges. Pin C triangles in place on top and bottom of design and B triangles to sides of design, keeping all outer edges even; tack. Topstitch ¼″ from block edges all around.

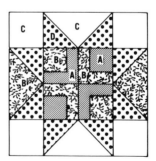

Block I

3a. Assembling sachet. Cut 3½″ square fabric piece for sachet back. Press ends of eyelet piece ¼″ to wrong side. Baste eyelet around sachet front (Block I), right sides together, so straight edge of eyelet is even with outer edge of block; overlap ends. Pin sachet front and back right sides together, and stitch ¼″ from edges all around, leaving 2″ opening in one edge for turning and stuffing;

turn to right side. Stuff sachet with cotton balls sprinkled with potpourri oil. Turn raw edges ¼" to inside; slip-stitch opening closed.

3b. Assembling box. Cut a 3½"-square cardboard template. Use template to mark squares on fabrics: Mark five squares on fabric A (for box sides and bottom) and six squares on fabric B or C (for lining of box and lid). Cut out squares along marked lines.

Carefully trim ⁵⁄₁₆" from each side of template. Pin three layers of batting together and treat as one thick layer. Holding template against batting, cut 11 squares of equal size. Using template, cut five additional cardboard pieces.

To make box sides and bottom, pin A pieces against five lining pieces, right sides together and edges aligned. Pin assembled Block I against remaining lining piece, for box lid.

Stitch each lining and fabric pair together on three sides, leaving ¼" seam allowances, to form six "pockets." Clip across corners; turn to right side. Insert a cardboard piece into each pocket. Insert a batting piece on each side of cardboard in four pockets, using knitting needle to poke batting into corners. Stuff lining side of fifth pocket (box bottom). Turn raw edges of pockets ¼" to inside; slip-stitch openings closed.

Arrange sides (S) and bottom (B) on work surface as shown in diagram, lining side up. Using doubled thread, whipstitch side and bottom edges together. Place lid on box, matching edges. To hinge, slip-stitch the slip-stitched edge of lid to both outside and inside of box.

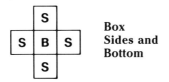

Box Sides and Bottom

Referring to photograph, glue a piece of satin cord, cut to fit, around lid edges, starting and ending at center back. Glue cord around remaining box edges.

3c. Assembling change purse. Cut four 5" × 5¼" fabric pieces for purse front, back, and two lining sections. On wrong side of one piece (front) mark a 3½" square centered between 5¼" edges and 1" from one 5" edge (top); baste along lines of square to mark right side of fabric.

Mark a 3" square centered inside first square, leaving ¼" fold allowance on each side. Cut away smaller square and clip into fold allowance at corners. Press inner edges to wrong side along basting; baste ⅛" from folds.

Place assembled Block I face up on work surface. Referring to photograph, place purse front on top, face up and with wider margin at top, so that block is centered in opening; pin and baste.

Pin lining sections to purse front and back, wrong sides together; baste. Topstitch purse front just inside basting line through all thicknesses. Press top edges ¼" to lining side; baste. Pin Velcro® half to each lining ⅛" below fold and centered between side edges; topstitch close to long edges through all thicknesses. Pin purse front and back right sides together, and stitch sides and bottom, leaving ¼" seam allowances. Zigzag-stitch along raw edges to prevent ravelling; turn to right side.

Billfold

1. Cutting, marking, and folding fabric. From fabric A, cut 7¼" square for backing. On right side of piece, mark off a 3½" square in each bottom corner to form two block outlines; do not cut out. Make one Block I patchwork on each marked square, referring to directions for Sachet, but without cutting additional backing squares.

2. Assembling billfold front. From fabric A, cut two 1¼"-wide strips, one 3½" long and one 7¼" long. Press lengthwise edges of strips ¼" to wrong side. Referring to photograph, center 3½" strip between blocks, overlapping raw edges ¼" at sides and matching raw edges at top and bottom; baste. Topstitch strip close to folds.

Pin 7¼" strip across piece, overlapping top of blocks ¼" with one folded edge and matching raw edges at ends; top-stitch along folded edges.

3. Lining. From fabric B, cut 7¼"-square for lining. From fabric B or C, cut two 7¼" × 6½" pieces for pockets.

From interfacing, cut three pieces: one 7¼" square, and two 7¼" × 3¼" pieces.

Baste interfacing square to wrong side of lining square. Press pockets in half lengthwise, right sides out, to form two 7¼" × 3¼" rectangles. Insert matching interfacing into each pocket with edges even; baste. Baste a pocket to each lengthwise edge of lining (top and bottom), matching raw edges. Pin right side of lining/pockets against right side of backing; stitch together ¼" from edges, leaving 4" opening in top edge for turning. Clip across corners. Turn to right side with pockets facing lining. Turn raw edges ¼" to inside; slip-stitch opening closed. Fold billfold in half as shown.

Key Ring

1. Marking, cutting, and folding fabric. Referring to directions for Sachet, make a miniature Block I using 1" square and 1¼" × 2" templates; make 2" square backing. Cut 2"-square piece for key ring back. From same fabric, cut 1"-wide bias strip to fit around key ring, plus ½".

2. Assembling key ring. Pin backing to block, wrong sides together; baste close to edges.

Cut ribbon in half to make two 2" lengths. Align ribbons, one on top of the other, and baste one end to block at center of one edge (top) with raw edges even; leave other end free.

Press one long and one short edge of bias strip ¼" to wrong side. Beginning at center top with raw end, pin strip around block, right sides together and raw edges even; overlap ends. Stitch strip in place ¼" from raw edges, being careful not to catch free ribbon ends with stitches. Turn strip to back of piece, miter corners, and slip-stitch in place, tucking free ribbon ends under fold before stitching center top. Working through all four layers, stitch across ribbons at top of key ring to secure.

Pincushion

1. Marking, cutting, and folding fabric. Following General Directions for cutting and folding, make one Block II, using two templates, a 2" square and a 2" × 4½" rectangle. Referring to photograph and illustration for color scheme, cut four squares from fabric A, eight each from B and C, and four rectangles from D. Fold pieces to form four triangles from A pieces, four squares and four triangles from B's, eight squares from C's, and four strips from D's.

2. Backing. Cut 4½" fabric square for backing. Use pencil to lightly mark horizontal and vertical center lines on right side of backing.

3. Assembling block. Referring to diagram and working from center outward, assemble block. Pin four C squares to backing, so that folded corners meet at center. Using double-threaded needle, tack centers and outer corners to backing. Pin four B squares in place, overlapping center squares, so that corners are ¼" from center of design and outer squares extend ¼" beyond first squares; tack down corners as before. In similar manner, attach four C squares over B's. Pin A triangles in place as shown, overlapping squares, so that points are ½" from center and outer edges are even with outer C's; tack.

Pin two D strips to top and bottom of design, overlapping outer pieces ¼" with folded edges; raw edges should be even with backing; tack. Attach two D strips to sides of design in same manner. Pin B triangles over center of strips as shown with outer edges even; tack. Topstitch ¼" from block edges all around. Assemble pincushion as for Sachet, except stuff with crushed potpourri.

Block II

Covered Boxes with Special Appeal

The nice thing about covered boxes is that they can be used again and again. When given as a gift with edible contents, for example, the box remains as a lasting remembrance, making the gesture all the sweeter.

EQUIPMENT: Compass.

MATERIALS: Discarded packages, such as the cigar box, tea and coffee tins, and cookie tins used here. Wrights upholstery braids and ribbons (see individual directions). Cotton fabric where indicated below. Can of "Scotch" Spra-Ment adhesive. Tube of "Scotch" Super Strength adhesive.

General Directions

Cover containers with fabric or wide ribbon trims; lay trims side by side to cover a wide surface. Adhere fabric by spraying wrong side with Spra-Ment adhesive and pressing on container. Cut off excess, with ends overlapping slightly. Decorate with velvet ribbon, upholstery braid, etc., adhering with Super Strength adhesive. For cans, put on lid before adding trim near upper edge.

Cigar Box

Cover entire box with 2¼"-wide ribbon trim. Use one piece for outside perimeter, one piece for inside perimeter, and three pieces for inside bottom. For lid, cut three long pieces, center on lid lengthwise, then carry ends to inside lid to meet in center. Glue ¼"-wide ribbon around upper and lower edges of box and on front edge of lid. Add ribbon to inside upper edges of box. Glue on frog to close, as shown.

Coffee Can

From fabric, cut piece the height and circumference of can, plus ¼" for overlap at top and bottom. Cut circle the diameter of can's lid, plus ¼" for rim. Adhere fabric to can and to lid. In crisscross pattern, glue lengths of ¼"-wide ribbon around outside of can; glue ribbon around bottom and near top edges.

Tea Tin

Cover tin with five 1"-wide lengths of ribbon, with edges all meeting in center of one side. Cover lid with three pieces of ⅞"-wide ribbon, alternating with two pieces of ¼"-wide ribbon. Glue ¼"-wide ribbon around edge of lid. Cover seam of box and top and bottom edges with ¼"-wide ribbon.

Large Cookie Tin

Cover sides and lid with fabric as for coffee tin. Glue braid around edge of lid. Glue two strips of braid, side by side, across lid as shown; edge with ¼"-wide ribbon. Glue two appliqué roses on lid. Glue ¼"-wide ribbon around bottom and near top edges.

Small Cookie Tins

Cover boxes with 2¼"-wide ribbon trim, using one piece for perimeter and three pieces for lid. Trim in various ways, as shown in photograph. For round box, braid is glued to bottom and near top edges; three lengths of braid cover raised edge of lid. For octagonal box, ⅝"-wide velvet ribbon is glued to top and bottom of box side, and ¼"-wide velvet ribbon is glued to lid, covering seams; edge of lid is finished with fringed braid.

Silhouette Appliqués in Three Guises: Picture, Tote, and Pillow

These accessories retain the charm of the old-fashioned paper silhouettes that inspired them. Although they would fit into almost any background, the colors can easily be modified to coordinate with any setting.

SIZES: Picture, 8½″ × 10¼″, unframed; pillow, 12½″ × 14½″; tote, 10½″ × 12″ × 4″ deep.

MATERIALS

General Materials: Use only cotton or cotton-blend fabrics and refer to photograph for additional information on colors and prints. 9″ black cotton or cotton-blend fabric square for silhouette. Fusible interfacing. Thread to match all fabrics.

Picture: Large scraps small windowpane check print for wall and small floral print for floor. Orange scrap for window. Blue scrap for sky. Floral print scrap for curtains.

Pillow: ½ yard windowpane check print for pillow and appliquéd floor. Large floral print scraps for wall and border. Solid brown and green scraps for wall sconce. Three different print scraps for rug. Polyester fiberfill.

Tote: Large print scraps for wall and floor. Solid brown scrap for table. Orange scrap for lamp base. Orange/brown print scrap for shade. ½ yard blue calico for tote lining. ½ yard 45″-wide beige corduroy.

General Directions

1. Making the patterns. Using sharp, colored pencil, draw lines across patterns, connecting grid lines. Enlarge patterns by copying design on paper ruled in 1″ squares. Solid lines of pattern indicate appliqué outline, dash lines indicate machine embroidery. Trace a separate appliqué pattern for each piece, including wall and floor. Use individual appliqué patterns to mark outlines on right side of appropriate fabrics, referring to photograph and materials lists for colors, and proceed as follows.

2. Marking, cutting, and joining wall and floor. For background, mark and cut out wall and floor pieces, adding ¼″ seam allowances around edges. Stitch wall to floor, right sides together and matching raw edges, and leaving ¼″ seam allowances. Press seam allowances toward the darker fabric. Using

enlarged complete pattern, dressmaker's carbon, and dry ball-point pen, transfer all design lines to right side of pieced background. Set aside.

3. Interfacing the appliqués. Cut a piece of interfacing slightly smaller than each fabric scrap for remaining appliqués, including border for pillow. Following manufacturer's directions, fuse interfacing to wrong side of each scrap.

4. Marking and cutting remaining appliqués. Mark outlines of individual appliqués on right side of scraps. Cut out appliqués along marked outlines, using small sharp scissors; cut out all interior spaces indicated by shading on patterns.

5. Appliquéing and finishing the project. Pin appliqués to background in marked positions, following directions for each project that follows. Machine baste 1″ in from marked outlines of each appliqué. Set sewing machine for close zigzag satin stitch. Using matching thread, satin stitch around each appliqué over machine basting, covering raw edges; zigzag lines may overlap in small areas. After all pieces have been appliquéd, machine embroider over or within dash lines,

Each square = 1″

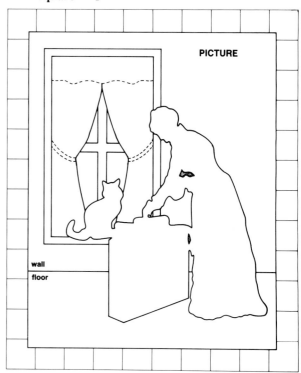

using close zigzag satin stitches and following directions for color under specific project. After all stitching is complete, trim away any threads or raw edges as necessary, then finish, following directions for individual project.

Picture

Cut and piece background and appliqué design, following General Directions. For window, appliqué sky, window frame, and curtains to background in that order. Machine embroider curtains, using matching thread making two rows of stitching for each tie-back. Mat and frame as desired.

Pillow

1. Cutting and marking fabric. From windowpane checked fabric, cut floor and two 3″ × 15″ pieces for pillow front and back. Cut wall piece (background) and mark design on it, following General Directions.

2. Cutting and appliquéing the design. Center and baste wall section on pillow front. Cut and appliqué designs to wall section and

pillow front, following General Directions and in this order. Pin and machine baste concentric ovals of rug to one another, then pin rug in place on pillow front. Pin silhouette and sconce in place, following pattern.

Satin stitch edges of rug sections, skipping over silhouette; satin stitch around silhouette, candle holder, and reflector.

Pin border to pillow front, overlapping edges of wall section, and satin stitch in place along inner and outer edges.

Using overlapping rows of satin stitches, machine embroider white candle and red flame. Using black thread, machine embroider spinning wheel spokes and thread from spool.

3. Finishing pillow. Place pillow front and back, right sides together with edges aligned, and stitch leaving ¼″ seam allowances and an opening for turning. Turn to right side; stuff with fiberfill until plump. Fold edges of opening ¼″ to inside, then slip-stitch closed.

Tote

1. The appliqué. Cut and piece wall and floor and appliqué design pieces to them following General Directions. Using brown thread and closely spaced narrow zigzag stitches, machine embroider top of lamp shade. Using black thread, satin stitch embroidery hoop in woman's hand; fill in center fabric section with overlapping rows of blue satin stitch.

2. Cutting the front and back and attaching the appliqué section. Referring to tote diagram, cut two 14½″ square pieces from beige corduroy for tote front and back; make sure nap runs in the same direction for both pieces. Cut away shaded areas shown on diagram. Center appliqué section on right side of one piece 1″ below top (front). Straight stitch appliquéd section in place ¼″ from edges; trim fabric to ⅛″ of stitching. Using narrow blue zigzag satin stitches, stitch around appliquéd section, covering machine stitching and raw edges.

3. Joining the front and back. Stitch tote front and back right sides together along

Each square = 1″

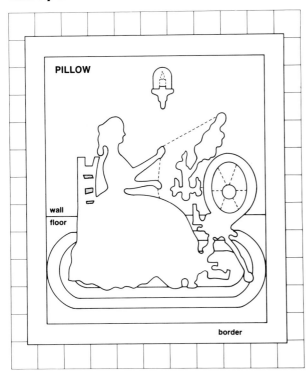

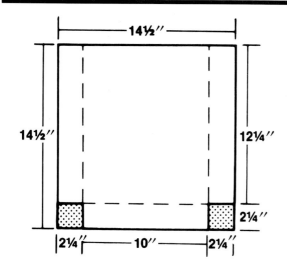

Tote Diagram

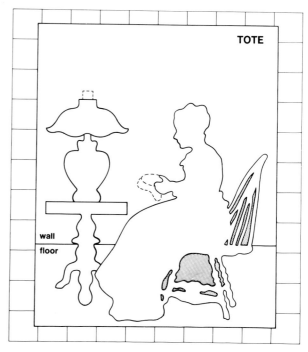

Each square = 1″

bottom edges and then along the sides, leaving ½″ seam allowances. Press open seam allowances. Fold notched edges right sides together at each corner, matching seams; stitch across each seam, making boxed corners. Fold and baste raw top edges of tote ¼″ to wrong side.

4. The straps. Cut two 12″ × 1½″ strap sections from corduroy. Press lengthwise edges of each ¼″ to wrong side, then fold in half lengthwise, wrong sides together, aligning pressed edges; top stitch lengthwise close to folded edges to join them.

Mark top center front and center back edge of tote with pin. Measure and mark with pins 2¼″ to left and right of each pin. Pin one strap to each side of tote so inner edges of strap touch outer pin markings and both ends of straps are ¼″ below folded top of tote; baste in place.

5. The lining. From blue calico, cut and assemble lining same as for tote. Insert lining into tote, wrong sides together, and aligning seams and top edges; slip-stitch securely together around top, enclosing straps. Topstitch ⅛″, then ¼″ from top edges all around.

6. Shaping tote. To accentuate boxed shape, crease bag and lining 2″ away from side seams on bag front and back, as indicated by vertical dash lines on diagram. Top stitch ⅛″ in from creases, catching and securing the lining to corduroy. In same manner, crease and stitch bag bottom along both long edges (horizontal dash lines) and ends, making 4″ × 9½″ boxed bottom.

Country-Style Patchwork and Appliqué Pillows, and a Knitted Duck Family

The traditional Star-and-Cross Pattern (left) and Snow Crystals (right) provide bold accents on two patchwork pillows, while an appliquéd and embroidered rooster and three hens make charming companions on the other two pillows. Mother duck and her ducklings are knitted in garter stitch to make cuddly friends for an infant or toddler.

Star-and-Cross Patchwork Pillow

SIZE: 15″ square.

EQUIPMENT: Graph paper. Thin, stiff cardboard.

MATERIALS: Closely woven cotton fabrics: small amounts unbleached muslin, yellow calico, and red calico; two 15½″ square pieces, one for lining and one for pillow back. 1¾ yards red welting. Matching sewing threads. 15½″ square piece batting. Fiberfill.

1. Making templates. Following Piecing Diagram, mark patch patterns on graph paper: A—1¾″ square. B—mark 5⅜″ square and divide in half for triangle pattern. C—mark 2½″ square and divide in half for triangle pattern. D—mark 1¾″ × 5⅜″ rectangle; on one long side, mark point 1¾″ from end; draw diagonal line from point to nearest corner, for shape shown. E—mark 1¾″ × 8″ rectangle; mark midpoint at one end and a point ⅞″ from this end on each long side; connect points for shape shown. Glue graph paper to cardboard; let dry; cut carefully along marked lines to make five templates.

2. Marking and cutting out patches. Using templates, mark patches: Place each template on wrong side of fabric, with right angles on straight of goods. Draw around template with sharp pencil held at an outward angle. Mark as many patches as needed of one color at one time, leaving ½″ between the patches.

On yellow calico, mark five of A, four of B, and eight of C. On red calico, mark eight of D. On muslin, mark four of A and four of E. Cut out each patch ¼″ outside pencil lines for seam allowances; pencil lines will be stitching lines.

3. Joining the patches. To join patches, place two pieces right sides together and stitch along line; press seam to one side, under darker color. Referring to Piecing Diagram, join A pieces in rows, then join rows for the nine-patch center. Join C's to D's, then C-D strips to E's for four corner pieces. Join two corner pieces to center and two to B's. Join three pieces for pillow front, which

should measure 15½″ square, including unused seam allowance around edge.

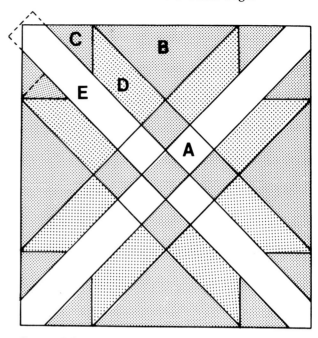

Star-and-Cross Piecing Diagram

4. Quilting. Place lining and pillow front wrong sides together with batting between them and baste together. Using matching threads, and referring to *How to Quilt* section at the back of the book, quilt on each patch, close to seam.

5. Assembling pillow. Trim welting if necessary so seam allowance measures ¼″. Pin welting to right side of pillow back, matching raw edges, rounding corners, and overlapping ends 1″; baste along seamline. Snip out 1″ of cord from one end of welting; cut away ¾″ of casing from other end; insert one end into other, turning in outer raw edge. Place pillow back and front right sides together, enclosing welting; stitch just inside basting line, leaving opening on one side for turning. Turn pillow to right side, stuff fully, and slip-stitch closed.

Snow Crystals Patchwork Pillow

SIZE: 13¾″ square.

EQUIPMENT: See Star-and-Cross Patchwork Pillow.

MATERIALS: Closely woven cotton fabrics: small amounts black, red, and black/red calico; two 14¼″ square pieces, one for lining and one for pillow back. 1⅔ yards red welting. Matching sewing threads. 14¼″ square piece batting. Fiberfill.

1. Making templates. Following Piecing Diagram, mark patch patterns on graph paper: A—2″ square. B—mark 2″ square and divide in half for triangle. C—mark 3¹¹⁄₁₆″ × 1⁹⁄₁₆″ rectangle; mark midpoint of each side; connect points for diamond with 2″ sides. D—2″ × 4″ rectangle. Glue graph paper to cardboard; let dry; cut carefully along marked lines to make four templates.

2. Marking and cutting out patches. To mark fabric, place each template on wrong side of fabric, with right angles of A, B and D and two parallel edges of C on straight of goods. Draw around template with sharp pencil held at an outward angle. Mark as many patches as needed of one color at one time, leaving ½″ between patches. On black, mark 20 of C. On red, mark 12 of C. On calico, mark 12 of A, eight of B, and four of D. Cut out each patch ¼″ outside pencil lines for seam allowances; pencil lines will be stitching lines.

3. Joining the patches. To join patches, place two pieces right sides together, and

stitch along seam line; press seam allowances to one side, under darker color. Referring to Piecing Diagram, join adjacent C pieces, sewing bias edges to straight edges. Sew A, B and D pieces between C sections for pillow front, which should measure 14¼″ square, including unused seam allowance around edge.

To finish pillow, see "Quilting" and "Assembling pillow" steps 4 and 5, for Star-and-Cross Pillow.

Appliquéd Hen and Rooster Pillows

SIZE: Two 12″-square pillows.

MATERIALS: Medium-weight cotton fabric: ¾ yard 36″-wide ecru; scraps of green, blue, red, and two different flower prints (see photograph). Polyester fiberfill. ⅜″-wide orange and red double-fold bias tape. Sewing thread: red, blue, green, orange, yellow, and white.

1. Making the patterns. Using pencil and ruler, draw lines across patterns, connecting grid lines. Enlarge patterns by copying designs on paper ruled in 1″ squares. Heavy lines indicate appliqués; fine lines and solid areas indicate embroidery.

2. Marking and cutting the fabric. From ecru fabric, cut four 12″ squares, two for pillow fronts and two for backs; set backs aside. Using dressmaker's carbon and dry ball-point pen, transfer hen pattern to right side of one pillow front; turn pattern, and transfer rooster to other pillow front. Referring to photograph and using pattern, transfer appliqués to colored fabrics; mark embroidery lines and solid areas on appliqués.

3. The appliqué. Following directions for *How to Appliqué* at back of book, cut out pieces and machine-appliqué to pillow tops. Set machine for ¹⁄₁₆″-wide zigzag stitch and embroider fine lines on appliqués in colors shown. Fill in solid areas with embroidery as follows: Remove pressure foot and lower feed dogs; set stitch-width dial to "0." By moving entire piece in circles, fill in solid areas on

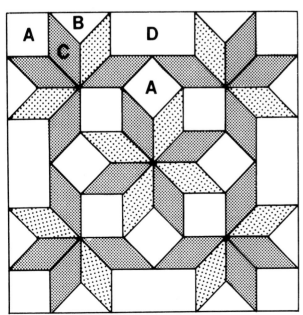

Snow Crystals Piecing Diagram

HEN PATTERN

ROOSTER PATTERN

Each square = 1"

pattern with stitching, overlapping stitches and filling in area until solid.

4. Assembling the pillows. To make each pillow, pair top and bottom with edges even and wrong sides together. Stitch pieces together ¼" from edge all around, leaving 4"-long opening for stuffing. Stuff pillow firmly with fiberfill; stitch opening closed.

Place each pillow with top up and finish edges with red or orange bias tape as follows: Unfold one edge of a 50" length of bias tape and pin along pillow edge, right sides together and raw edges aligned; overlap ends where they meet; fold top end ¼" to wrong side. Stitch tape to pillow edge along crease all around. Refold tape to enclose raw edges; turn pillow over and stitch close to creased edge of tape all around.

Knitted Duck Family

SIZES: Mother Duck, 5" high; Medium Duck, 4" high; Duckling, 3" high.

MATERIALS: Worsted-weight yarn, small skein yellow or white for each body, small skein brown for eyes. Gold or tan felt with matching thread for bill and feet. Knitting needles No. 6 (4¼ mm). Plastic eggs: 4" long for Mother Duck, 3" long for Medium Duck, and 2½" long for Duckling. Small piece of calico print for bonnet. Small amount of stuffing for heads and tails. Pinking shears.

GAUGE: 9 sts = 2" (garter st).

Mother Duck

Cast on 38 sts.

Rows 1-5: * K 1, p 1, repeat from * across.

Rows 6-8: Knit.

Row 9: Inc 1 st in first st, k across, inc 1 st in last st—40 sts.

Row 10: Knit.

Rows 11, 13, 15, 17, 19, 21, 23, and 25: Repeat row 9—56 sts.

Rows 12, 14, 16, 18, 20, 22, 24, and 26: Knit.

Rows 27, 28, 29, and 30: Bind off 10 sts at beg of row, k across.

Row 31: Repeat row 9.

Row 32: Knit.

Row 33: Repeat row 9.

Rows 34-44: Knit. Bind off remaining sts, leaving long yarn end for sewing.

Finishing: Trace pattern for bill onto felt, fold bill in half and sew in place, centering fold between rows 28 and 30. With brown yarn, embroider eyes in satin stitch. (See *Embroidery Stitches.*)

Fold duck in half, sew head, back, and sides. Trace pattern for feet onto felt, fold and overcast cut edges and attach at front of duck, extending feet and leaving back opening large enough to insert egg. Stuff head and tail; insert egg.

Bonnet (Mother Duck only): With pinking shears, cut a 6½" diameter circle. Gather outer ½" edge to fit head, attach yarn ties.

Medium Duck

Cast on 36 sts.

Rows 1-5. * K 1, p 1, repeat from * across.

Rows 6-8: Knit.

Mother Duck Bill
Medium Duck Bill
Duckling Bill

Fold

Actual-Size Patterns

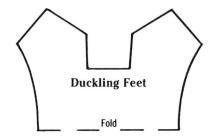

Duckling Feet

Fold

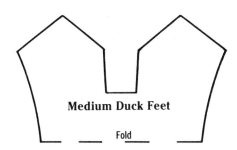

Medium Duck Feet

Fold

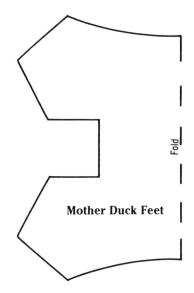

Mother Duck Feet

Fold

Row 9: Inc 1 st in first st, k across, inc 1 st in last st—38 sts.

Rows 10, 12, 14, 16, 18, and 20: Knit.

Rows 11, 13, 15, 17, and 19: Repeat row 9—48 sts.

Rows 21 and 22: Bind off 8 sts at beg of row, k across.

Rows 23 and 24: Bind off 9 sts at beg of row, k across—14 sts.

Row 25: Repeat row 9.

Rows 26-34: Knit. Bind off remaining sts, leaving long yarn end for sewing.

Finishing: Complete same as for Mother Duck, sewing bill between rows 23 and 24 and eliminating bonnet.

Duckling

Cast on 26 sts.

Rows 1-3: * K 1, p 1, repeat from * across.

Rows 4-8: Knit.

Row 9: Inc 1 st in first st, k across, inc 1 st in last st—28 sts.

Row 10: Knit.

Rows 11, 13, and 15: Repeat row 9—34 sts.

Rows 12, 14, and 16: Knit.

Row 17: Bind off 12 sts at beg of row, k across.

Row 18: Repeat row 17.

Row 19: Repeat row 9.

Rows 20-26: Knit. Bind off, leaving long yarn end for sewing.

Pillow Clouds

Dream on a cloud with one or more of these heavenly pillows or pillow covers. Made of silky fabrics and splashed with stars and/or rainbows, each pillow front is appliquéd and then quilted.

MATERIALS

General Materials (for all): Fabric scraps of taffeta, silk, satin, rayon or other shiny materials in peach, gold, aqua, mint green, lilac, and tan (see photograph), or ⅛ yard of each color for all rainbows and stars. **(Note:** The rainbow fabrics differ from one another for added texture. Blanket binding, ribbons, etc., could be used in combination with yard goods and scraps.) Polyester batting for quilting pillow front. Polyester fiberfill for stuffing. White sewing thread.

Blue square pillows (to make two): ¾ yard 45"-wide sky blue satin. ¾ yard 45"-wide white lightweight cotton for lining and inner pillows. ¼ yard 36"-wide white satin or taffeta, or one 11" × 14" piece, for corner clouds. Two 10" zippers (optional).

Cloud-shaped pillows: ½ yard 45"-wide dotted aqua satin fabric, for aqua pillow. ⅝ yard 45"-wide white-on-white striped satin-like fabric, for large white pillow front. ¾ yard 45"-wide solid white satin fabric, for large white pillow back and boxing strip, and small white pillow front and back. ¾ yard 45"-wide lightweight cotton for lining.

General Directions

1. Making patterns. Using sharp, colored pencil, draw lines across pattern, connecting grid lines. Enlarge patterns by copying on paper ruled in 1" squares. Solid lines are stitching lines; dotted lines indicate where pieces overlap; dash lines indicate extra quilting lines.

2. Marking and cutting pillow front and back. Trace complete pillow design. Place tracing-paper pattern on right side of fabric for pillow front with carbon between; go over lines with tracing wheel (or dry ballpoint pen) to transfer complete design, including perimeter of pillow (do not transfer dash lines). Remove pattern and carbon. Cut out pillow front, adding ½" all around for seam allowance. For pillow back, pin front to pillow back fabric, wrong sides facing; cut out back.

3. Marking and cutting appliqué pieces. Trace each separate appliqué piece, including overlaps. Position appliqué patterns on right side of appropriate fabrics with carbon between; transfer appliqué shape; remove pattern and carbon. Cut out each piece, adding ¼" all around each outside edge for seam allowances (add ½" to straight edges of corner clouds on square pillows). For each rainbow, trace and cut each piece from a different color rainbow fabric.

4. The appliqué. Make complete rainbows of the five colors as follows, to create one appliqué piece. Arrange rainbow pieces together as shown in photograph, overlapping stitching lines. Baste and stitch together, following directions for machine appliqué in *How to Appliqué* section at back of book and using the closest and widest zigzag setting. Baste whole rainbows, then stars and clouds in place on pillow fronts, overlapping stitching lines. Stitch to pillow fronts, as directed in *How to Appliqué* section.

5. Quilting. When appliqué is completed on the pillow front, cut one piece each of batting and lightweight cotton lining the same size and shape as pillow front. Pin lining to wrong side of pillow front with batting between; baste. Starting with centermost part of design, straight-stitch around appliqués as directed for each pillow, stitching through all layers. Treat each rainbow as one piece. Adjusting basting if necessary, stitch around pillow perimeter leaving ½" seam allowances.

6a. Making the knife-edged pillow. Stitch pillow front and back right sides together leaving ½" seam allowances and a large opening on one side. Insert a 10" zipper if desired. Turn to right side; insert inner pillow (see directions below for Inner Pillow). Turn in seam allowance along raw edges; slipstitch closed.

6b. Making the pillow with boxing. Piece strips together end to end, leaving ½" seam allowances, to make one long strip for boxing, following individual pillow directions for width; make strip as long as circumference of pillow, plus 2". With right sides together and raw edges flush, pin and baste one long edge of boxing strip around pillow front. Pin ends of boxing strip together, 1″ from ends and right sides together. Stitch boxing strip to pillow front leaving ½″ seam allowances; stitch ends together and trim to ½″. With right sides together, pin raw edge of boxing strip and edges of pillow back together, making sure that the shape of the cloud back lines up with the cloud front; stitch as before, but leave 5″ opening for stuffing. Clip seam allowances, turn, and stuff fully. Turn in raw edges of opening; slip-stitch closed.

7. Making inner pillows. Cut two pieces of lightweight cotton 2″ wider and longer than pillow. Stitch pieces right sides together leaving ½″ seam allowances and opening at center of one side. Clip seam allowances at corners; turn and stuff fully. Turn in raw edges; slip-stitch closed.

Blue Square Pillows

Size: each, 12″ square
Using patterns and following General Directions, transfer design and cut pillow front and back from sky-blue satin. Cut three corner clouds from white satin, five rainbow pieces, and one star (for pillow with star) from tan fabric. Assemble rainbows. Appliqué all pieces to pillow front; before stitching corners of clouds, trim overlapped portions of rainbows close to cloud stitching line. Quilt pillow front, stitching around rainbow, clouds, and all around star (for pillow with star). Make pillow following General Directions for Knife-Edge Pillow.

Aqua Cloud Pillow

Size: 18″ × 14″
Using patterns and following General Directions, transfer design and cut pillow front and back from dotted aqua satin fabric. Cut two gold, two white, and one tan star. Appliqué stars to pillow front. Quilt pillow front, stitching around each star. From aqua fabric, cut 2½″-wide strip and piece for boxing strip (about 53″ plus 2″). Make pillow, following General Directions for Pillow with Boxing.

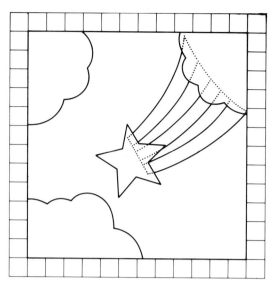

Blue Square Pillows   Each square = 1″

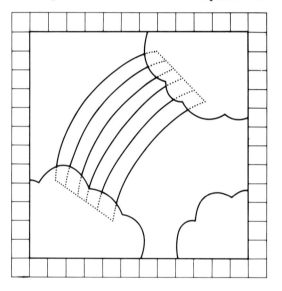

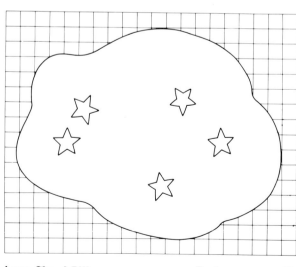

Aqua Cloud Pillow   Each square = 1″

Large White Cloud Pillow

Size: 21¼" × 17½"

Using patterns and following General Directions, transfer design and cut one piece from white-on-white striped satin for pillow front; cut one piece from solid white satin for pillow back. Cut five rainbow pieces and three gold stars. Assemble rainbow and appliqué all pieces to pillow front. Quilt pillow front, stitching around rainbow and stars; extend lines from rainbow as indicated by dash lines, to suggest clouds. From solid white fabric, cut 3"-wide strips and piece for boxing strip (about 72" plus 2"). Make pillow, following General Directions for Pillow with Boxing.

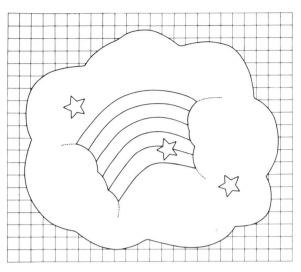

Large White Cloud Pillow   **Each square = 1"**

Small White Cloud Pillow

Size: 13½" × 10"

Using patterns and following General Directions, transfer design and cut two pieces from solid white satin fabric. Cut five rainbow pieces and one gold star. Assemble rainbow and appliqué pieces to pillow front. Quilt pillow front, stitching around rainbow and outer edge of star; extend lines from rainbow as indicated by dash lines, to suggest clouds. Make pillow, following General Directions for Knife-Edge Pillow.

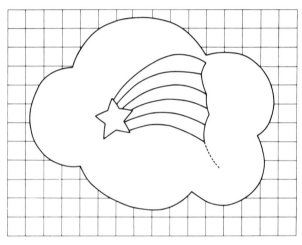

Small White Cloud Pillow   **Each square = 1"**

From dolls to picture frames, pot holders, and a handsome needlework design, these creations come straight from the heart.

Bride and Bridesmaid Dolls

SIZE: 8″ tall.

EQUIPMENT: Compass. Knitting needle. Size 1 crochet hook (for Spring Maid).

MATERIALS (for each doll): Scrap of flesh-colored felt. Six-strand embroidery floss:

red, yellow, and blue. Orange-colored pencil. Yellow fingering yarn for hair. Flesh-colored sewing thread. Pipe cleaner. Fiberfill. **For Bride:** 15″ square white satin. 20″ × 34″ piece fine white netting (bridal illusion). Scrap of white felt. 2¼ yards 2″-wide white galloon lace. ¼ yard ¼″-wide white satin ribbon. ¾ yard ⅛″-wide baby blue satin ribbon. Seed pearls. Six blue-and-white fabric forget-me-nots. Three white roses for headpiece. Six white daisies cut from embroidered lace. White sewing thread. White craft glue. **For Spring Maid:** 15″ square red polka dot fabric. Scrap of red felt. ¾ yard 2½″-wide white cluny lace. ½ yard ¾″-wide embroidered ribbon trim. 1 yard ¼″-wide blue satin ribbon. ¼″ yard ½″-wide white pre-gathered lace. Tiny basket of forget-me-nots and leaves. Red and blue sewing thread. For bonnet: White crochet thread. ¾″ plastic ring. **For Valentine Maid:** 15″ square black satin. Scraps of red and black felt. ½ yard 4½″-wide white eyelet lace. ¼ yard 1½″-wide white eyelet lace. 1 yard ¼″-wide red satin ribbon.

General Directions

Trace patterns, completing half patterns indicated by long dash line. Make separate patterns for body, bodice, and heart. Using compass, make a 3¾″-diameter circle for base pattern. Cut out felt and fabric pieces as directed below; do not add seam allowances. Unless otherwise indicated, machine-stitch pieces right sides together as close to outside edges as possible, using matching thread. When stitching trims in place, fold ends under ¼″ and overlap in back.

1. Doll's body and bodice section.
Using patterns, cut two body and four arm sections from flesh-colored felt. Also cut two felt bodices from white for Bride, red for Spring Maid, and black for Valentine Maid. Lay each bodice over each body piece and zigzag or topstitch along neckline. Mark position of face on one body piece (front). Using three strands of embroidery floss in needle, embroider eyes in blue and mouth in red, using a single French knot for each. See *Embroidery Stitches* at back of book. Color cheeks as shown, using orange-colored pencil. Stitch arm pieces right sides together in pairs, leaving straight ends open. Insert a 3″ piece of pipe cleaner into each arm. Place body pieces together, embroidered and bodice sides facing out. Insert an arm ¼″ into body at each shoulder; pin so that arms extend outward,

perpendicular to body. Stitch body pieces together through all thicknesses, starting at bottom of one side, working up and around, and leaving bottom open. Stuff body with fiberfill, using knitting needle.

2. The hair. Cut thirty 6″-long strands of fingering yarn. Working in groups of six strands and using two strands of yellow embroidery floss in needle, tack groups through center to head, working from top of forehead to back of neck. Divide hair into two sections and tack each section to side of face, encircling strands; finish hair for each doll as directed.

3. The skirt. Cut base, using pattern made earlier. Cut 6″ × 15″ strip(s) for skirt. Fold skirt in half crosswise, wrong side out; stitch short edges together leaving ¼″ seam allowances; press open seam allowances. Baste around skirt tube ¼″ from each edge. At one edge (bottom), pull basting thread, gathering to fit outside edge of base. Stitch skirt bottom to outside edge of base, right sides together, just inside basting. Turn skirt right side out and stuff firmly with fiberfill. Gather top edge closed, and tie off.
Finish dress, following individual directions. With skirt seam at back, place bottom of doll body over top of gathered skirt and slip-stitch securely in place. Conceal joining with ribbon belt as directed.

Bride

1. Doll's body and dress. Refer to General Directions to make body and dress. Cut base and skirt from white satin; cut another skirt from netting. Baste skirt pieces together, and make skirt. Cut two 1 yard lengths of 2″-wide lace. Baste each ⅜″ in from top edge and gather to measure 18″. Slip-stitch lace around bottom of skirt in overlapping tiers as shown in photograph. Baste leftover lace piece ¾″ from top edge and gather to fit neckline. Fold lace lengthwise along basting to make two tiers and slip-stitch to neck of bodice with shortest tier on top. Stitch doll body to skirt, following General Directions. Tie white satin ribbon around waist with bow at back.

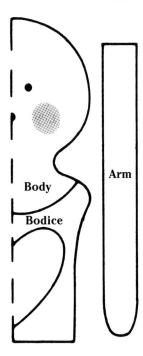

Body

Bodice

Arm

Doll Patterns (actual size)

2. The hair. Divide hair on each side into three parts and braid. Pull braid ends to top of head as shown in photograph and tack in place using embroidery floss.

3. Finishing touches. Thread a needle with white thread and knot one end. String a necklace of pearls long enough to fit doll and tie around neck; trim thread ends. For veil, cut an 8″ × 22″ strip of netting and baste ¼″ from one long edge; gather to 1½″ and tack three roses to gathered edge, stems facing raw edge. Slip-stitch veil to hair as shown, concealing ends of braids.

Cut baby blue ribbon into three 9″-long streamers. Tie streamers in bows around stems of forget-me-nots to make bouquet. Glue daisies to ends of streamers. Bend arms so that hands meet in front of body and stitch bouquet to hands.

Spring Maid

1. Doll's body and dress. Refer to General Directions to make body and dress. Cut base and skirt from polka dot fabric. Make skirt. Baste ¼″ from top of 2½″-wide lace and gather to fit bottom of skirt. Slip-stitch around skirt, so that bottom edge touches ground, as

shown in photograph. Conceal top edge of lace by slip-stitching embroidered ribbon around skirt as shown. To bodice front and back, slip-stitch pre-gathered lace in a "V" from shoulders to center of waist. Slip-stitch blue ribbon to lace edge. Tie a small blue bow and tack to bodice front as shown. Stitch doll body to skirt, following General Directions. Tie 9″ piece of ribbon around waist with bow at back.

2. The hair. To finish hairdo, trim ends of hair and tack two small bows at sides of head as shown.

3. The bonnet. Using crochet hook and thread, crochet bonnet as follows.

Row 1: Sc over ring 48 times.

Row 2: Sc in each st around; join with sl st, ch 2.

Row 3: Sc in first 4 sts, then 2 sc in next st, repeat this pattern around. Join with sl st, ch 2.

Rows 4-6: Sc in each st around; join with sl st and ch 2.

Rows 7-9: Sc in each st; inc 4 sts evenly spaced in each row.
 Tie 6″ length of blue ribbon into bow and tack to back of bonnet. Tack bonnet to head as shown. Bend arms so that hands meet in front of body and stitch basket to hands.

Valentine Maid

1. Doll's body and dress. Refer to General Directions to make body and dress. Cut base and skirt from black satin. With right sides up, place 4½″-wide eyelet on top of skirt so that top edge is even with one long (top) edge of fabric; baste ¼″ in from top edge and short side edges. Make skirt. Baste 1½″-wide eyelet ¼″ from top edge and gather to fit neckline. Fold lace lengthwise along basting and slip-stitch to neck of bodice (folded edge to inside) as shown in photograph. Stitch doll body to skirt, following General Directions. Tie a 9″ length of ribbon around waist with bow at back. Cut remaining ribbon into equal pieces and make four small bows; tack at intervals around skirt as shown.

2. The hair. To finish hairdo, pull two sections to top of head and tie together. Trim ends as shown to make bun. Using 12 strands of yarn, make 3″ braid; slip-stitch around base of bun, overlapping ends in back. Bend arms so that hands meet in front of body. Using pattern, cut heart from red felt and tack to hands.

Valentine Frames

EQUIPMENT: Cardboard. X-acto knife.

MATERIALS

Felt frame: Purchased clear plastic 5″ × 7″ box-type picture frame. Felt: 9″ × 12″ red sheet; assorted color scraps. 5″-square piece yellow gift-wrap or other shiny paper.

Eyelet frame: Purchased clear plastic 3½″ × 4½″ picture frame with easel stand. 5″-square piece red construction paper. 5″-diameter round white paper lace doily. ½ yard ⅞″-wide white pre-gathered eyelet trim. ¼ yard ⅜″-wide pink ribbon.

For Both: Spray adhesive. White glue for plastics, such as Elmer's® Craft Bond II. Clear tape.

1. Making the patterns. Trace each actual-size half pattern (A, B, and C for Felt Frame; B only for Eyelet Frame), completing each by reversing for second half. Glue tracings to cardboard; cut out patterns when dry.

2a. Felt frame. Remove inner box from frame; set aside. Cut 8″ × 10″ rectangle from red felt. With long edges at top and bottom, place pattern A on felt so that heart is 1¾″ from left short edge and centered between long edges; mark around heart. Also mark a 1⅜″ square in each corner. Cut away heart and corner squares.

Using spray adhesive, glue felt to frame. Cut 10 small hearts from assorted felt scraps, using pattern C; glue to frame front as shown in photograph, using white glue.

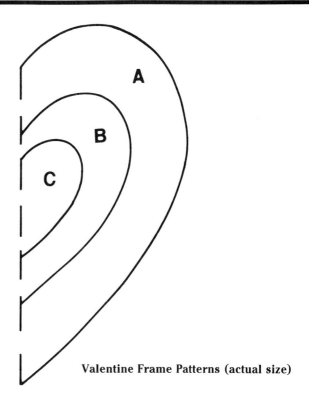

Valentine Frame Patterns (actual size)

For mat, mark heart B, centered, on yellow paper; cut out and discard. Tape mat to inside of frame so that cutouts are concentric. Center desired photograph behind mat; tape in place. Replace inner box.

2b. Eyelet frame. Beginning and ending at bottom right corner of frame, use white glue to attach eyelet trim all around, so that lace extends ¾″ beyond frame edges, as shown in photograph; overlap ends. Tie ribbon into bow; glue to cover lapped ends.

For mat, glue doily, right side up and centered, to construction paper, using spray adhesive; let dry. On wrong side, mark a 3½″ × 4½″ rectangle, centered. With short sides of rectangle at top and bottom, center pattern B within rectangle; mark around outline. Cut away margins and heart, using X-acto knife. Insert mat into frame. Insert desired photograph behind mat.

Hearts and Flowers Needlepoint

SIZE: 8¼″ square.

EQUIPMENT: Masking tape. Tapestry needle. Artist's wooden stretcher strips to make 12″ × 12″ frame. Staple gun and staples.

MATERIALS: 12"-square piece 10-mesh-to-the-inch white mono needlepoint canvas. Paternayan Paterna 3-strand Persian yarn: one 8-yard skein each red and white, small amounts of purple, yellow, and green; see color key. Heavy cardboard for mounting. Straight pins.

1. Preparing frame and canvas.
Assemble stretcher frame, following manufacturer's directions. Read *How to Needlepoint* section at back of book. Prepare canvas as directed. Measuring 2" in and 2" down from upper right corner, mark position of first stitch with pin. Staple canvas to frame, so that threads are straight and taut.

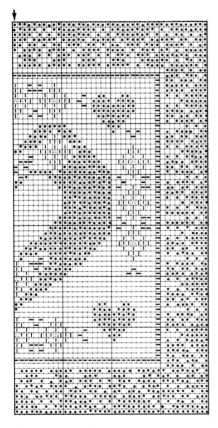

Needlepoint Chart

⊞	Purple #640
⊟	Green #527
⊡	Red #200
☐	White #001
⊡	Yellow #441

2. The needlepoint.
Chart is given for right half of design. Each symbol or blank square on chart represents one needlepoint stitch; different symbols represent different colors.

Starting at pin and following chart and color key, work all stitches with two strands yarn in needle, working in continental or diagonal stitch. Work entire right side if desired, then work left side, reversing chart and omitting center vertical row marked by arrow, or work across in rows from top to bottom in same manner. When charted design is finished, work four rows with white all around red border.

Remove completed needlepoint from frame and block if necessary.

3. Mounting needlepoint.
After canvas has been blocked, stretch it over heavy cardboard cut same size as needlepoint design. Hold canvas in place with straight pins pushed partway into edge of board through canvas. Check needlepoint to make sure rows of stiches are straight. Carefully push (or hammer) pins in the rest of the way. Fold excess canvas to back of board; tape in place. Frame as desired.

Crocheted Heart Pot Holders

SIZE: 7" × 7".

MATERIALS: Coats & Clark O.N.T. Speed-Cro-Sheen, 1 100-yard ball of red and white for each pot holder. Steel crochet hook No. 1. ¼ yard decorative ribbon. 7" square soft interlining fabric.

GAUGE: 5 sc = 1"; 6 rows = 1".

Pot Holder

With red or white, ch 2.

Row 1: 3 sc in 2nd ch from hook. Ch 1, turn each row.

Row 2: 2 sc in first st, sc in next st, 2 sc in last st—5 sc.

Rows 3-11: 2 sc in first st, sc in each sc to last st, 2 sc in last st—23 sc.

Row 12: Sc in each sc across.

Row 13: Inc in first and last sc—25 sc.

Rows 14-21: Repeat rows 12 and 13 alternately—33 sc.

Rows 22-29: Sc in each sc across—33 sc.

Shape First Half:
Row 30: Sc in each of 16 sc. Ch 1, turn.

Row 31: Repeat row 30.

Row 32: Sc in each of 14 sc, dec 1 sc by working last 2 sc tog. Ch 1, turn each row.

Row 33: Sc in each of 13 sc, work last 2 sc tog—14 sc.

Row 34: Work first 2 sc tog, finish row—13 sc.

Rows 35-37: Work to last 2 sc, work last 2 sc tog—10 sc.

Row 38: Sc in each sc. End off.

Shape Second Half:
Row 30: Join yarn in center st of row 29, sc in each of next 16 sc. Ch 1, turn.

Row 31: Repeat row 30.

Row 32: Work first 2 sts tog, finish row.

Row 33: Repeat row 32.

Row 34: Work across, work last 2 sc tog.

Rows 35-37: Work first 2 sc tog, finish row—10 sc.

Row 38: Sc in each sc. End off.
  Make another piece the same.

Finishing: Cut interlining same shape as crocheted pieces. Using Speed-Cro-Sheen, blanket-stitch crocheted pieces tog with interlining inside (see *Embroidery Stitches* section at back of book).

Edging: Join contrasting color at top center. Sc in blanket st, * ch 3, sc in next blanket stitch, repeat from * around. End off.
  Fold ribbon in half to form hanger. Sew ends to back of pot holder.

Quilted-Leaf Cachepots

For something quite different and handsome to hide the pots of your favorite house plants try these unusual quilted covers. Each one bears two different leaf patterns, so together they make a kind of garden all their own.

SIZES: 8″, 6″, and 4″-square cachepots.

MATERIALS: 1⅜ yds 45″-wide muslin (for three boxes). Thin, stiff cardboard. Polyester batting. Loose stuffing. Green sewing and embroidery threads.

1. Cutting and marking fabric. Cut five 5″ × 9″ pieces of muslin, for small box; five 7″ × 13″ pieces for medium box; and five 9″ × 17″ pieces for large box. Cut five 4″-, 6″-, or 8″-square pieces of cardboard for small, medium, or large box, respectively.

On four muslin pieces of appropriate size, lightly mark a 4″, 6″, or 8″ square at one end with tailor's chalk, leaving ½″ margin around three sides.

Using dressmaker's carbon and tracing wheel, transfer a leaf design of appropriate size within each marked square, repeating each leaf twice. (Two actual-size leaf patterns are given for each box.)

2. Quilting. For each muslin piece, including fifth piece cut a thin layer of batting as well as another 4″, 6″, or 8″ square of muslin for lining. Pin and baste batting and muslin lining squares, in that order, behind marked areas of larger muslin pieces, leaving ½″ margin on three sides.

With green sewing thread, machine-stitch along marked leaf design, to quilt.

3. Finishing side and bottom pieces. Turn long side edges of piece ½″ to underside; press. Fold piece in half crosswise, wrong sides together. Slip-stitch folded side edges together; press. Insert a cardboard square of appropriate size inside pocket made. Stuff loose filler into pocket on both sides of cardboard, concentrating filler towards center of square. Fold open edges of pocket to inside, edge of leaf side first, then edge of plain side; slip-stitch closed.

4. Assembling box. When all five pieces of a box have been completed, place together as shown in piecing diagram, leaf side up (A and B indicate different leaf patterns, C is plain bottom). Using two strands of green floss in needle and cretan stitch (See *Embroidery stitches* at back of book), embroider A-C and B-C edges together. To form box, fold A and B sides so they touch; using cretan stitches, embroider adjacent sides of A and B pieces together.

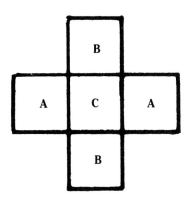

Box Sides and Bottom

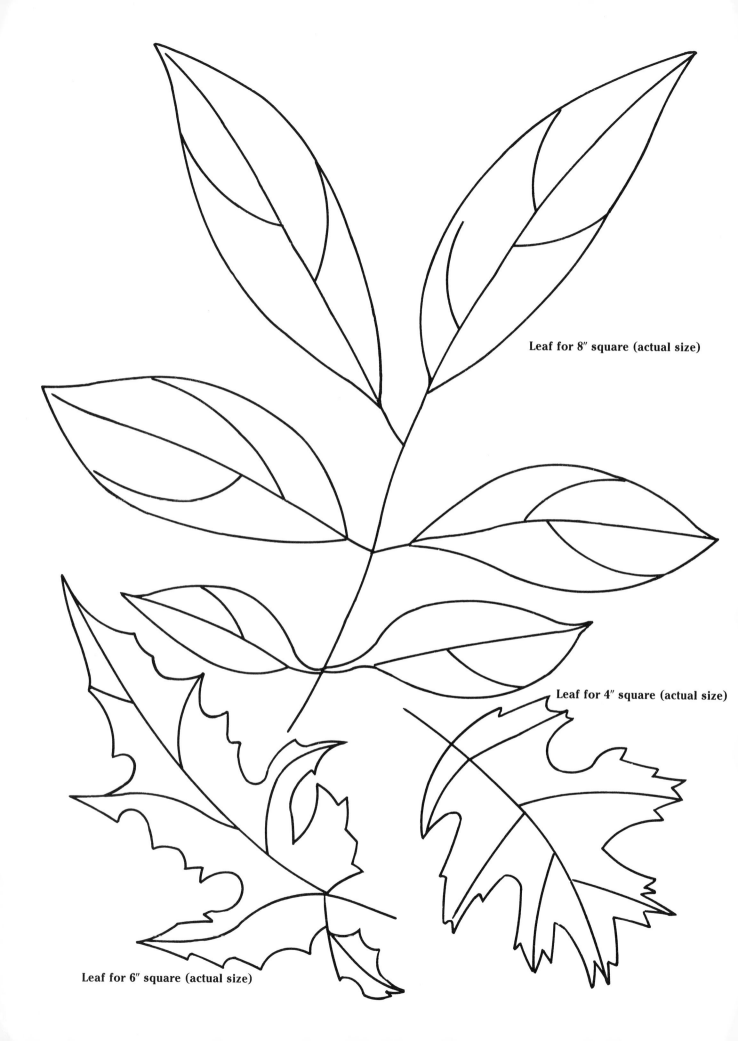

Leaf for 8″ square (actual size)

Leaf for 4″ square (actual size)

Leaf for 6″ square (actual size)

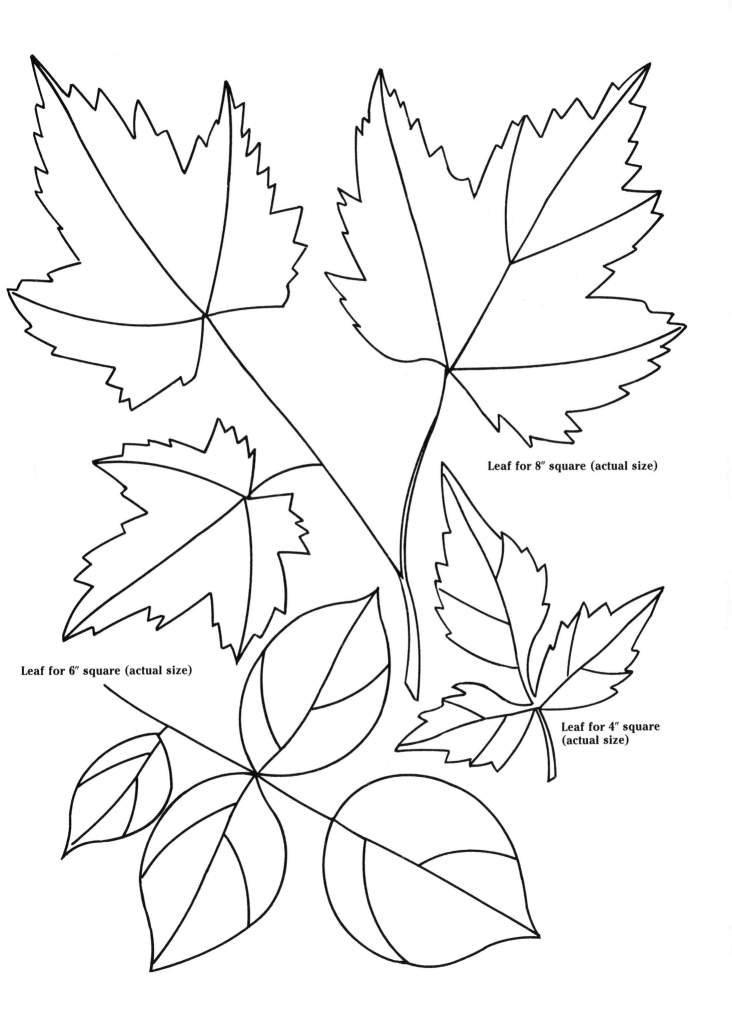

Leaf for 8″ square (actual size)

Leaf for 6″ square (actual size)

Leaf for 4″ square
(actual size)

Cat Family Draft Stopper

A draft under a door can easily be eliminated with this parading family of machine-appliquéd cats on a sand-filled base.

MATERIALS: ¾ yard 44″-wide closely woven, rust-colored cotton. Small amounts of closely woven cotton in gold calico, tan calico, black, gold, and orange. Sewing thread: orange, black, brown, green, and white. Polyester fiberfill. Sand.

1. Making the patterns. Connect grid lines of pattern given here. On paper ruled in 1″ squares, copy outline of cat's body and fine-lined facial details only. On paper ruled in ½″ squares, copy all lines of cat, including spots.

2. Cutting the fabric. Following directions for *How to Appliqué,* at back of book, and omitting spots, transfer small cat pattern to gold, tan calico, black, and gold calico fabrics. Transfer spots to orange fabric. Transfer large cat to gold calico. Cut out all pieces.

Cut two 13″ × 41″ pieces from rust fabric.

Draft Stopper Cat Pattern
Scale for mother cat = 1″   Scale for kittens = ½″

3. Appliquéing and embroidering cats. On right side of one rust fabric piece, pin cats in order shown in photograph, with hind paw of each 1″ from bottom edge, nose of mother cat ½″ from left edge, and hind leg of last kitten 3¼″ from right edge. Pin spots on gold kitten.

Using orange thread and ⅛″-wide zigzag stitches, machine appliqué all cats but black in place, including legs, outer ear lines, and mouth of mother cat.

Using 1/16″-wide zigzag stitches, appliqué orange spots and embroider mouths of the three light kittens. Using black thread, appliqué black cat and satin stitch all noses. Straight stitch white whiskers on black cat, and black whiskers on rest of cats. Using green thread, satin stitch all eyes green. Using brown thread, satin stitch inner ears of mother cat.

4. Joining front and back. Turn appliquéd fabric, wrong side up so cats face right. Using yardstick and ruler, mark stitching line ½″ in from edge of bottom and left side. Mark line across top parallel to bottom line and from left side to large cat and just above kittens' tails. Continue line around mother cat's profile to upraised paw. Use ruler to mark straight line from paw to bottom.

Pin front and back pieces right sides together. Stitch along marked line, leaving large opening along straight end. Trim seam allowances to ½″. Clip into seam allowances along curves, and clip corners. Turn piece to right side, and poke out corners with knitting needle. Firmly stuff mother cat with fiberfill. Stuff kittens with fiberfill or sand, as desired. Turn under ½″ seam allowances at open end, and slip-stitch opening closed.

Autumn Wreath

A straw wreath decked with autumn-colored fabric leaves, bows, and wheat adds a festive note to Fall. The wreath would enhance any door, wall, or tabletop, and the individual leaves can also be used as drink coasters. As coasters, the leaves would look equally attractive in lovely shades of green for year-round use.

SIZE: 14″ in diameter.

MATERIALS: ¼ yard each of the following 36″-wide solid-color cotton fabrics: gold, medium brown, light brown, and orange; ½ yard 36″-wide tan calico; ¼ yard 36″-wide gold calico; polyester batting; a ready-made 14″-diameter straw wreath; brown thread; straight pins; fusible webbing; fine-gauge wire; adhesive tape; 20 assorted dark and light wheat stalks; a large T-pin.

EQUIPMENT: Knitting needle, pinking shears.

1. Preparing the pattern and cutting the leaves.
Draw lines across the pattern given here to complete the grid. On white paper, rule a similar grid of ½″ squares. Draw in the half-leaf pattern.

Fold the gold calico in half lengthwise, right sides together. Using dressmaker's carbon and a dry ball-point pen and aligning the dash line of the pattern along the fold of the fabric, trace four leaves. Adding ¼″ around the outlines for seam allowances, cut out the leaves. Similarly, trace and cut out the following leaves: four of tan calico, four each

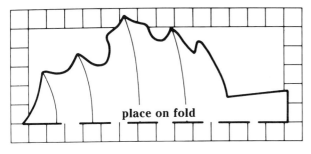

Leaf Pattern place on fold **Each square = 1″**

of solid gold and dark brown, two of solid orange, two of solid light brown, and ten of batting.

2. Stitching and attaching the leaves.
To make each leaf, pin two matching fabric pieces right sides together, center a batting leaf over them, and stitch together, leaving ¼″ seam allowances and an opening across the end of the stem. Turn the leaf right side out, poking out the corners with a knitting needle. Using the leaf pattern as a visual guide, topstitch the four crosswise veins and central vein of the leaf.

Overlap the ten leaves, mixing the colors and facing the leaves in the same direction, and pin each one in place on a straw wreath, using a straight pin at both ends and leaving a quarter of the wreath uncovered at the top, as shown.

3. The bows and wheat.
Cut six 27″ × 2¾″ strips as follows: two of solid orange fabric, two of tan calico, and two of fusible webbing. Using a strip of the webbing between them and right sides out, iron the matching fabric strips together following the manufacturer's directions. Trim the edges of each strip with pinking shears. Form a bow out of each strip by folding both ends across the middle, place one bow on top of the other, set them at the center of the open space at the top of the wreath, and anchor them in place by wrapping fine-gauge wire over their centers and around the wreath. Secure the wire and pull the bow loops up to cover it.

Tape the wheat stalks together around the middle and anchor them behind the bow with a T-pin stuck through the tape.

PART III
FOR CHILDREN ONLY

From nursery accessories to toys, to furnishings for the room of an older child, this section provides many projects that are suitable for both girls and boys. There are rag and sock dolls, stuffed animals, and decorative accents, such as a matching quilt and pillow set, a photo album with a cross-stitched cover, and a choice of wall hangings.

Storybook Rag Dolls

Surprise a special child with a loveable Little Bo-Peep, Jack and Jill, Little Red Riding Hood, or Little Boy Blue. The dolls' bodies are all identical, but they are finished and dressed differently.

GENERAL MATERIALS: ⅓ yard 36″-wide pink cotton fabric (enough for two dolls). Red crayon or rouge for coloring cheeks. Cotton batting for stuffing. All-purpose glue. (Additional materials in individual directions.)

General Directions

1. Making patterns and marking and cutting fabric. Enlarge patterns by drawing designs on paper marked with grid of 1″ squares; complete half and quarter-patterns indicated by long dash lines. Short dash lines indicate folds; dotted lines indicate stitching. When cutting out body and garment pieces, add ¼″ for seam and hem allowances on all edges unless otherwise indicated; do not, however, add allowances when cutting felt. For each doll, cut two head-body pieces and four separate legs (reversing pattern for two legs) of pink fabric.

2. The features. Using carbon, transfer features to one head section. Using two strands of floss in needle, embroider features. Use outline stitch for eyebrows, some mouths, and to outline eyes as shown in photograph. Fill in eyes and some mouths using satin stitches (shading on pattern indicates direction of stitches). See *Embroidery Stitches* at back of book. Color girls' cheeks with rouge or crayon.

3. Assembling doll. Place head-body pieces right sides together; pin and sew, leaving bottom open. For each leg, sew front and back sections right sides together, leaving top ends open. Clip seam allowances along all curves. Turn all pieces to right side. Stuff arms first, then stitch along dotted lines to close. Stuff head-body and each leg fully. Turn under bottom edges of body and sew closed. Turn under top edges of legs and sew legs to body, with leg seams centered.

Jack

ADDITIONAL MATERIALS: 6-strand brown and pink embroidery floss. ½ ounce dark brown knitting worsted. Small amounts of cotton fabric: red, blue-and-white checked gingham, and white stretch fabric. Scraps of red, yellow, and blue felt. Sewing thread to match all fabrics and yarn. Four tiny white buttons. 14″ length narrow blue ribbon. Small red pompon from ball fringe.

1. The doll's body. Make and assemble body following General Directions, but embroider brown eyes and eyebrows and pink mouth.

2. The hair. For hair, fold about forty 5″-long strands of brown yarn in half and tack at mid-point across back of head to cover; make second layer above first to thicken. Place about fifty 6″-long strands of yarn across top of head in two layers; stitch across at one side. Glue down strands at sides; trim in front.

3. The shirt. Cut one back and two fronts. Sew shirt sections right sides together at shoulders and sides; hem sleeves, collar, and front edges. Sew buttons at X's.

4. The pants. Cut two pants sections of red cotton. Sew right sides together from A to B and B to C, on both sides. Hem edges; sew on 1″ red square for pocket. Fold square gingham handkerchief in pocket. Tack straps together at shoulders; sew on buttons. Gather back waist to fit (dotted line on pattern).

5. The socks and shoes. Cut socks of stretch fabric. Fold in half; sew side and bottom edges together. Turn top edge under; tack sock to leg. For each shoe, cut sole, upper, and strap of blue felt. Fold upper in half; whip ends together and upper to sole.

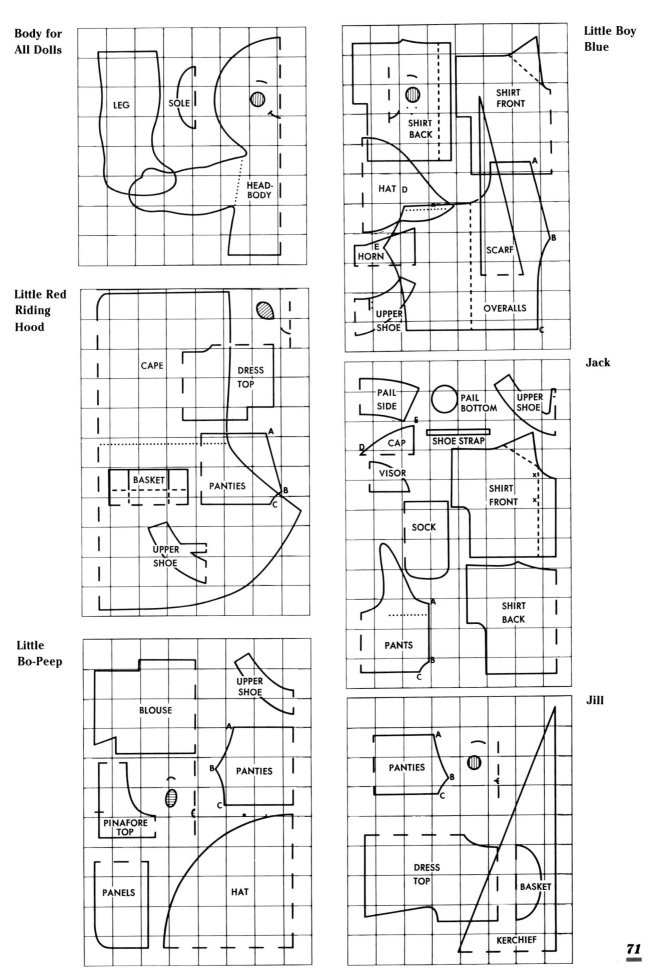

**Body for
All Dolls**

LEG SOLE

HEAD-
BODY

**Little Red
Riding
Hood**

CAPE

DRESS
TOP

A

BASKET PANTIES

B
C

UPPER
SHOE

**Little
Bo-Peep**

BLOUSE

UPPER
SHOE

A

B PANTIES

C

PINAFORE
TOP

PANELS HAT

**Little Boy
Blue**

SHIRT
FRONT

SHIRT
BACK

A

HAT D

SCARF B

E
HORN

UPPER
SHOE

OVERALLS

C

Jack

PAIL
SIDE

PAIL
BOTTOM

UPPER
SHOE

SHOE STRAP

D
CAP

VISOR

SHIRT
FRONT

x
x

SOCK

SHIRT
BACK

A

PANTS

B
C

Jill

A

PANTIES

B
C

DRESS
TOP

BASKET

KERCHIEF

71

Each square = 1″

Fold center flap of upper shoe under; tack. Insert strap to fold; tack ends to sides.

6. The cap. For cap, cut five pieces and two visors of red felt. Whip the five pieces together from D to E to form crown. Whip the two visors together along curved edges. Sew visor under crown edge. Tack on pompon. Stuff cap lightly with cotton and tack to head, gathering edges slightly.

7. The pail. For pail, cut bottom, side, and ¼″ × 2″ strip for handle from yellow felt. Whip pail together along sides and whip bottom to side; tack on handles. Glue pail to hand.

Jill

ADDITIONAL MATERIALS: 6-strand bright blue, red, and brown embroidery floss. ½ ounce rust brown knitting worsted. Cotton fabrics: ¼ yard yellow; small amounts plain white, stretch white, white dotted Swiss, blue-and-white stripe. Red and yellow felt. ½ yard ¼″-wide white ribbon. Four tiny white buttons. Red and yellow baby rickrack. Tiny artificial flowers.

1. The doll's body. Make and assemble body following General Directions, but embroider blue eyes, brown eyebrows, and red mouth.

2. The hair. For hair, cut about thirty 27″ strands of yarn. Arrange in two layers across back of head; stitch across yarn down center of head. Tack hair to each side on back of head. Bring strands from one side over top of head and down opposite side; repeat with strands on other side. Arrange on top and front of head; sew across to continue part line to front. Gather strands at sides into bunches; tie each bunch with white ribbon.

3. The panties. Cut two pantie sections of white cotton. Sew pantie sections together from A to B and B to C, on both sides. Hem legs and waist. Gather at waist to fit.

4. The petticoat. Cut 3″ × 18″ piece dotted Swiss; sew ends together. Hem edges; sew lace around one edge, gather other edge to fit doll's waist.

5. The dress. Cut dress top in one piece from yellow cotton. Fold in half and sew underarm and side seams together. Slash down half-pattern line on one side (back) from neck to bottom. Hem neck and sleeves.

For skirt, cut 3″ × 26″ piece yellow fabric and sew ends together. Hem one edge; gather and sew other edge to dress top. Gather sleeves ½″ from ends. Put dress on doll; overlap back edges, fold under top edge, and sew closed.

6. The apron. Cut 2¾″ × 7½″ piece for skirt, 1½″ square for pocket, 2″ × 3″ piece for bib, two 1″ × 9½″ pieces for ties, one 1″ × 7″ piece for neck strap. Sew pocket and red and yellow rickrack to skirt. Gather skirt to width of bib, hem all raw edges, and attach bib to skirt. Hem ties and neck strap and sew on. Sew buttons to strap ends.

7. The socks and shoes. Make socks of white stretch fabric and shoes of red felt as for Jack, using his patterns. Sew button on each outer side of shoe strap.

8. Finishing touches. Cut yellow kerchief; hem edges.

Cut two basket pieces from yellow felt; whip together around outer edges. For base, roll up ¼″ × 15″ strip, glue and tack to center. For handle, tack ¼″ × 4½″ strip of felt to opposite sides of basket. Glue artificial flowers in basket; tack basket sides together where handles join. Glue handle around doll's wrist.

Little Bo-Peep

ADDITIONAL MATERIALS: 6-strand pink, turquoise, and brown embroidery floss. ½ ounce yellow knitting worsted. Cotton fabric: small amounts of flowered and white dotted Swiss. 2 yards white lace edging. 2 yards pink velvet ribbon. Yellow baby rickrack. Bright pink and turquoise felt. Two 6″ pipe cleaners. Tiny artificial flowers.

1. The doll's body. Make and assemble body following General Directions, but embroider turquoise eyes, pink mouth, and brown eyebrows.

2. The hair. Cut about seventy 9″ strands of yellow yarn. Arrange in two layers around head. Stitch across top center to form part. Drape yarn over front of head for bangs and trim. Glue side and back hair down.

3. The blouse. Cut two blouse sections of dotted Swiss; sew, right sides together, at shoulders and sides. Slash down half-pattern line on one side (back). Hem neck and sleeves. Tack lace edging to sleeves. Gather neck and sleeves ¼″ from edges. Put on doll. Overlap back edges, turn under top edge, and sew closed.

4. The panties and petticoat. Cut two pantie sections from dotted Swiss. Sew as for Jill. Tack on edging. For petticoat, cut 2½″ × 20″ dotted Swiss and make as for Jill.

5. The pinafore. Cut pinafore top from flowered fabric. Fold in half; sew underarm seams from crossline to bottom. Slash down center back (at half-pattern line). Hem neck and armhole edges.

For pinafore skirt, cut 3″ × 30″ piece flowered fabric; hem one long edge. Sew remaining long edge to top, gathering to fit. Sew rickrack around bottom of skirt, as shown in photograph. Put pinafore on doll; overlap back edges, turn under top edge, and sew closed. Cut two panels for sides of skirt from dotted Swiss. Hem edges and trim edges with lace. Gather at top ½″ from edge and tack to each side of pinafore at waist. Tie pink ribbon around waist.

6. The hat. Cut hat of flowered fabric; hem edges and trim with lace. Gather 1″ from edge all around. Trim edge with bow and flowers. Stuff cotton into crown, and tack hat to head.

7. The shoes. Cut two uppers and two soles (use pattern for Jack's sole) from pink felt. Fold uppers in half and whip ends of each together; whip upper to each sole. Tack ribbon bow to each shoe, securing shoe to foot at same time.

8. Finishing touches. For crook, twist two pipe cleaners together to measure 9″. Cut 1″ × 9″ piece of turquoise felt. Wrap around pipe cleaner and whip edges together. Bend into shape and tack to hand with ribbon bow and tiny flowers.

Little Boy Blue

ADDITIONAL MATERIALS: 6-strand brown, blue, pink, and tan embroidery floss. Yarn: ½ ounce yellow-gold knitting worsted; scrap of blue. Cotton fabric: scraps of blue, white, and red-and-white checked gingham; scraps of black-and-white stripe and red-and-white polka dot. Yellow and blue felt. ½ yard white braid. Two small hooks and eyes.

1. The doll's body. Make and assemble body following General Directions, but embroider blue eyes, brown eyebrows, pink mouth, and make tan freckles with French knots.

2. The hair. Make hair as for Jack.

3. The shirt. Cut one shirt front and two backs from white cotton. Sew sections right sides together, at shoulders and along sides. Hem sleeve, neck, and collar edges. Place shirt on doll; overlap back edges, turn under top edge, and sew closed.

4. The overalls. Cut two blue overall sections. Stitch them right sides together from A to B and D to E. Then fold sides at dash line and join front and back along underleg-crotch (C to B to C). Hem all edges. Topstitch with double strand of white thread as shown in photograph. For pocket, sew 1½″ square of blue cotton fabric to pants. For handkerchief, fold scrap of polka dot fabric into pocket. For striped patch, sew on 1″ ragged square. For straps, cut two 1″ × 5½″ pieces. Hem edges and topstitch. Sew straps to pants at X on pattern. Cross straps in back and fasten to front with hooks and eyes. Gather waist in back at dotted line to fit.

5. Accessories. Cut red-and-white checked scarf; hem edges and tie on.

For shoes, cut uppers and soles (use Jack's sole pattern) from blue felt. Whip ends of each upper together, then upper to each sole. Slash shoes and make holes where indicated. Lace blue yarn through holes for shoelace; tie bow.

Cut hat from yellow felt. Whip long sides together. Stuff lightly with cotton; glue on head. Glue on white braid hatband and knot ends.

Cut yellow felt horn. Whip long sides together. Stuff lightly with cotton. For horn handle, cut ¼″ × 3″ strip of yellow felt; glue around wrist; glue horn to handle.

Little Red Riding Hood

ADDITIONAL MATERIALS: 6-strand brown and red embroidery floss. Yarn: ½ ounce dark gold knitting worsted, scrap of red. Cotton fabric: small amounts of flower print, plain white, white stretch, white organdy, checkered scrap. 2 yards white lace. 12″ × 16″ piece red wool jersey. Two pompons from red ball fringe. Red and gold felt. Narrow white ribbon.

1. The doll's body. Make and assemble body following General Directions, but embroider brown eyes, red mouth.

2. The hair. Cut 37″ strands and make as for Jill. Braid at sides for 2½″; tack at this point; cut strands off 1″ from tacking. Tie on ribbons. Cut five 2″ strands; tack at midpoint to forehead for bangs.

3. Panties and petticoat. Make white cotton panties and petticoat as for Bo-Peep. Edge with lace.

4. The dress. Cut dress top in one piece from flowered fabric. Sew underarm and side seams. Slash down center back at half-pattern line. Hem neck and sleeve edges. Sew lace around neck.

For skirt, cut 2¾″ × 20″ piece from flowered fabric; make as for Jill and sew to dress top. Trim with red and yellow rickrack and lace at edge, as shown in photograph. Put dress on doll; overlap back edges, turn under top edge, and sew closed.

5. The apron. Cut 2¼″ × 9″ piece organdy. Hem one long edge and both ends. Gather raw edge to 3½″ length. For tie-waistband section, cut 1½″ × 21″ piece organdy. Hem; fold in half lengthwise, placing gathered edge of apron at center of fold. Stitch waistband to apron. Sew open edges of ties together.

6. Socks and Shoes. Make socks as for Jill.

For shoes, cut upper and sole (use Jack's pattern) from red felt. Whip ends of uppers together and soles to uppers.

7. The cape. Cut cape from red jersey. Fold in half along half-pattern line and sew seam at top to form pointed hood. Hem all edges. With large-eyed needle threaded with red yarn, make running stitches along dotted line; pull yarn to gather hood, and tie into bow. Tack a pompon at each end.

8. The basket. Cut gold felt basket. Cut into corners at solid lines; fold at dash lines and tack corners together. Stuff with cotton and cover with checkered fabric; tack fabric to basket. For handle, cut ¼″ × 4″ strip gold felt; tack ends to sides of basket. Glue handle around doll's wrist.

Winsome T-shirt and Sock Dolls

Nothing is more cuddly than a soft fabric doll and these have appealing personalities to boot. Made of T-shirt scraps or old socks and dressed in clothes that can be sewn in a jiffy, the dolls are economical as well.

T-shirt Dolls

SIZE: About 10″ high.

EQUIPMENT: Light weight cardboard. Compass. Embroidery scissors.

MATERIALS (for each doll):

Body: ¼ yard 36″-wide pink cotton knit fabric, or adult size T-shirt, for body. Large skein yarn in desired color, for hair. Sewing thread to match fabric and yarn. Small amounts 6-strand cotton embroidery floss in red, blue, brown, and black. Polyester fiberfill.

T-shirts and Panties: White and colored cotton knit. White lace.

Jeans: Denim. Gingham. String.

Overalls: Denim. Bright cotton fabric. 2 tiny round buttons.

Dress: Gingham or calico. Baby rickrack or pregathered lace trim.

Pinafore: White cotton fabric. Ruffled eyelet trim. White double-fold bias tape.

General Directions

1. Making patterns. Draw lines across patterns to connect grid lines. Enlarge

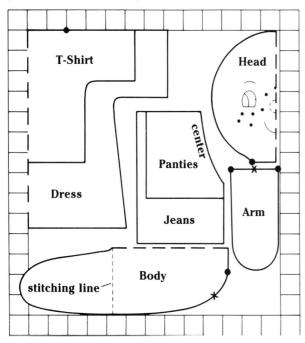

T-shirt Doll Patterns   **Each square = 1″**

patterns by copying designs on paper ruled in ½″ squares. Complete half patterns (indicated by long dash lines) by tracing over half pattern with pencil, folding pattern along dash lines and tracing firmly over back side of pencil lines.

2. Marking and cutting fabric. Following directions below for Doll and Clothes, transfer patterns, to wrong side of fabrics, using dressmaker's carbon and dry ball-point pen. Place pieces to be cut from same fabric ½″ in from fabric edges and at least ½″ apart. For cotton knit pieces, place patterns on doubled fabric, wrong side out, and transfer; stitch through both thicknesses as directed. For other fabric pieces, mark patterns on single thickness, reversing or flopping pattern for two of the four pieces required. Cut out all pieces ¼″ outside marked lines for seam allowances. Cut out additional pieces without patterns, following individual directions; seam allowances are included in dimensions given.

3. Stitching dolls. To sew, pin pieces right sides together with edges aligned and stitch along marked lines, leaving ¼″ seam allowances.

Doll

1. Making patterns and marking fabric. First, read through General Directions. On wrong side of doubled pink knit fabric, mark body, two arms, and head, omitting facial features. Stitch along marked lines, leaving straight edges between dots open. Cut out pieces as directed; turn to right side.

2. Stuffing body and attaching limbs. Stuff legs loosely to short dash line shown on pattern. Topstitch across body on that line. Stuff torso loosely. Turn neck edges ¼″ to inside; baste all around. Stuff arms, turn raw edges ¼″ to inside, and slip-stitch opening closed. Pin arms to body, matching X's. Pinch top of one arm, centering it over body side seam at X on one side and slip-stitch in place. Repeat to attach arm on opposite side.

3. Head. Transfer facial features to one side of head (front). Stuff head firmly. Roll a small amount of fiberfill into a ball for nose; insert under front and over stuffing under spot indicated on pattern for nose. Take a stitch at one side of nose, then run needle under nose to opposite side; pull tightly. Stitch all around the nose in this manner.

Whip-stitch raw neck edges closed. Insert neck ¼″ into body opening, matching side seams; stitch neck securely to body all around. Remove basting.

4. Embroidering face. Work with three strands of floss for all embroidery, and begin each length by knotting one end and running needle through head from front to back; tug thread gently so that knot passes through fabric and is embedded in stuffing. To end off, run needle through head from front to back; tug thread gently and clip excess.

Using stem stitches, make brown eyebrows, black outlines for eyes, and a red mouth. Work irises in blue satin stitch. Make brown French knot freckles. For stitch directions, see *Embroidery Stitches* at back of book.

5. Hair. Using compass, draw two 5″-diameter circles on cardboard with 1½″ hole in center; cut out discs and hole (see diagram). Place discs together and make a slit through both thicknesses as shown. Work through slit to cover discs with four or five layers of yarn.

Slip scissors between discs and cut all strands at outside edge of disc. Draw a strand of yarn between discs and wind very tightly around yarn; knot; remove discs. Fluff out yarn into a pompon.

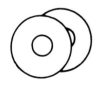

Making a Pompon

Use matching thread to stitch center of pompon to crown of head. Arrange strands evenly all around. Tack bottom layers to head, leaving top layers free. Finger comb strands downward from crown; trim.

Clothes (first read General Directions)

1. T-shirt. Using pattern, mark shirt outline on wrong side of doubled knit fabric. Stitch shoulders through both layers, leaving neck open between dots; stitch each underarm side seam. Cut out, leaving ¼″ seam allowances. Fold neck edges ⅛″ to wrong side twice; pin. Using running stitches and contrasting thread, hand stitch neck edges through folds all around. Turn bottom edge of shirt to wrong side and slip-stitch hem. Similarly, hem sleeve ends.

2. Jeans and overalls (for each doll). Cut four jean sections from denim, flopping two of them. Stitch pieces in pairs, right sides together, at center (see pattern), to form front and back. Stitch front and back together along inseams, making a continuous seam; stitch side seams; turn. Fold waist ¼″ to inside; top stitch ⅛″ from fold.

To fringe leg bottoms, pull crosswise threads for ¼″. For knee patches, cut 1″ squares from cotton scraps. Press raw edges under ⅛″. Slip-stitch to front of jeans or overalls, as shown in photograph.

Using all six strands of blue floss in needle, work seven ¼″-long vertical straight stitches around jeans for belt loops, centering them over topstitching, spacing them evenly, and securing each. Use needle to thread a doubled length of string through loops. Put jeans on doll. Tighten cord and knot. Trim and knot ends.

Cut from denim 1½″ × 2″ rectangle for bib and two 1¼″ × 4½″ straps. For bib, press all but one 2″ edge ¼″ to wrong side; topstitch ⅛″ from fold. Pin bib, right side out and centered, to inside of waist front, aligning the raw edges; stitch with invisible stitches.

Fold each strap lengthwise, right side out, so that edges overlap ¼″ at center back. Top-stitch close to lapped edge. Pin one end of each strap behind and ¼″ below top corner of bib; tack.

Stitch a button to each corner of bib, making stitches through all thicknesses to secure straps. Put overalls on doll, crossing straps in back and tucking free ends inside waist; pin. Remove overalls. Tack straps to waist.

3. Panties. Mark two panty outlines on wrong side of doubled cotton knit fabric. Stitch center seam of each through both layers, to form front and back. Cut out, leaving ¼" seam allowances. Assemble panties as for jeans. To finish, turn raw edges ⅛" to wrong side twice; slip-stitch. Cut lace to fit leg edges, plus ⅛"; slip-stitch in place lapping ends at inseam.

4. Dress. Cut two dress sections from gingham or calico fabric. Stitch at shoulders, right sides together, leaving neck opening between dots. Stitch remaining seams and hem raw edges. Cut rickrack or lace to fit neck and hem, plus ½". Stitch rickrack in place ⅛" from dress edges, overlapping ends at center back. Stitch neck lace in place with gathered edge even with neck edge, overlapping ends as for rickrack. Stitch hem lace to wrong side of hem, so that lace extends below hem as shown in photograph.

5. Pinafore. From cotton fabric, cut 3¼" × 4" rectangle for skirt. Press one long edge and both short edges ⅛" to wrong side twice; top-stitch. Gather raw edge to length of 2¼". Center gathered edge between long sides of bias tape (waistband and tie piece); pin. Unfold tie ends; press each under ⅛"; refold. Topstitch open edges of tie ends.

Cut two 4¾" lengths from eyelet trim for straps. Press strap ends under ⅛"; stitch. Put pinafore on doll, over dress. With bound edge of each strap toward center, tuck ends inside of waistband at front and back without crossing, and pin to waistband with bottom edges of strap and waistband even. Remove pinafore and stitch straps in place over top stitching.

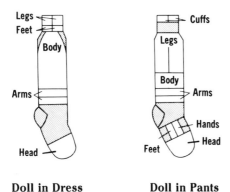

Doll in Dress   Doll in Pants

Sock Dolls

SIZES: 12" to 14" tall.

EQUIPMENT: Large darning needle. Knitting needle.

MATERIALS (for each): One patterned knee sock with at least 4" of solid color at toe and top. Scrap yarn or DMC pearl cotton for hair. 6-strand embroidery floss in contrasting color. Matching sewing thread. Scraps of ⅛"-wide ribbon (optional). Polyester fiberfill.

Doll in Dress

1. Cutting sock. Cut sock into pieces following diagram; discard shaded areas. Sizes of pieces will vary with sock; use entire solid colored portion of toe (or about 4") for head; cut limbs in matching pairs, either patterned or solid color. Turn pieces inside out and stitch together as directed below, leaving ¼" seam allowances.

2. The bodies and limbs. Stitch tapering sides of body closed, leaving both ends open; turn and stuff.

Stitch sides of each arm closed, tapering seams as you approach one end to meet hand; trim seam allowances; cut open other end. Turn right side out, using knitting needle, and stuff.

Fold each leg in half so ribbed edge is at one end, and stitch along side opposite fold; turn inside out. Roll up ribbed edge (top edge of sock) ½" for cuff and tack in place; stuff leg.

Fold each foot in half crosswise and stitch sides closed, leaving end open; turn and stuff. Insert open end of foot ¼" into cuff and slip-stitch all around.

Insert open end of legs ¼" into center bottom of body and slip-stitch in place; slip-stitch body closed on either side of legs to finish bottom of skirt.

Stitch arms to each side of body, turning in open edges.

3. The head. Stuff head with fiberfill. Baste around neck edge and pull thread, gathering to fit body. Turn under open edge of body section, insert head, and stitch all around.

Using two strands of embroidery floss, embroider eyes and mouth as shown in photograph, using different colored strands to make mouth. From discarded portion of sock, cut small circle for nose and stitch it to face.

4. The hair. Thread a large darning needle with yarn or pearl cotton. Take a stitch in top of head and draw a thread through almost to the ends of the strand, then take a back stitch. In the same spot, take another back stitch, this time catching the yarn around your finger as you pull it through to leave a loop or curl on the head. Continue making curls around head. If desired, attach small ribbon bows to sides of head.

To make braids, insert three strands of thread at the same spot, leaving 3″ ends dangling. Braid strands together and tie ribbon bow around ends.

Doll in Pants

1. Cutting the sock. Cut sock into pieces following diagram; discard shaded areas. Sizes of the pieces will vary with sock; use entire solid colored portion of toe (or about 4″) for head. Cut limbs in matching pairs, either patterned or solid color. Turn pieces inside out and stitch together as directed below, leaving ¼″ seam allowances.

2. The body and limbs. Stitch inseams of legs; turn and stuff.

Baste around one edge of body (top), and pull thread, gathering opening to about a 1″ diameter; stuff body. Slip-stitch bottom of body to legs.

Stitch sides of each arm closed, tapering seams as you approach one end for wrist; cut open both ends; turn and stuff.

Fold hands and feet in half crosswise; stitch along two sides, tapering to a closed end for tips and leaving other end open; turn and stuff. Turn in ends of arms and legs and insert hands and feet; stitch.

Fold cuffs crosswise and stitch ends together, making tube; turn and slip-stitch along raw edge to ankles (see green doll), or wrists (see black doll).

3. The head. Stuff head with fiberfill; baste around neck edge and pull thread, gathering neck to fit body. Turn under open edge of body, insert head, and stitch.

Using two strands of embroidery floss in the needle, embroider face as shown in photograph.

4. The hair. Make hair as for Doll in Dress.

Crocheted Mouse Family

Worked in single crochet and simply dressed, this happy mouse threesome can be created in no time for a favorite child.

SIZES: Adults, 8¼" high; baby, 6" high, including ears on all.

MATERIALS: One 4-ounce skein grey knitting worsted. Size G crochet hook. Stuffing. Glue. 6" square grey felt. 6" square pink felt or velour. Blue and black felt scraps. 6"-long piece of 4"-wide eyelet trimming. Heavy, waxed grey thread. 6-strand, bright pink embroidery floss. One small button. Two small gold safety pins. Scraps of cotton materials for clothes. 1 yard narrow white ribbon. Tracing paper.

GAUGE: 4 sc = 1"

Mother and Father Mouse

BODY: Beg at bottom, ch 2.

Rnd 1: 6 sc in 2nd ch from hook. Do not join rnds; mark end of ends.

Rnd 2: 2 sc in each sc.

Rnd 3: (Sc in next sc, 2 sc in next sc) 6 times—18 sc.

Rnd 4: (Sc in next sc, 2 sc in next sc) 9 times—27 sc.

Rnd 5: (Sc in each of 2 sc, 2 sc in next sc) 9 times—36 sc.

Rnds 6-11: Work even in sc.

Rnd 12: (2 sc in next sc, sc in each of next 3 sc) 9 times—45 sc.

Rnds 13-17: Work even in sc.

Rnd 18: (Sc in each of 3 sc, work next 2 sc tog) 9 times—36 sc.

Rnds 19-23: Work even in sc.

Rnd 24: (Sc in each of 4 sc, work next 2 sc tog) 6 times—30 sc.

Rnd 25: Work even in sc.

Rnd 26: (Sc in each of 3 sc, work next 2 sc tog) 6 times—24 sc.

Rnd 27: Work even in sc.

Rnd 28: (Sc in each of 2 sc, work next 2 sc tog) 6 times—18 sc.

Rnd 29: Work even in sc.

Rnd 30: (Sc in next sc, work next 2 sc tog) 6 times—12 sc.

Rnds 31 and 32: Work even in sc. End off. Stuff; leave neck open.

TAIL: Ch 6; sc in 2nd ch from hook and in each remaining ch—5 sc. Ch 1, turn each row. Work 4 rows even. Dec 1 st on next row. Work 4 rows even—4 sc. Dec 1 st on next row. Work 16 rows even—3 sc. Dec 1 st on next row. Work 10 rows even—2 sc. Work 2 sts tog. Work 5 rows even—1 sc. End off. Roll tail; sew edges tog. Sew tail to rear of body over rnds 6 and 7.

HEAD: Beg at tip of nose, ch 2.

Rnd 1: 4 sc in 2nd ch from hook.

Rnd 2: 2 sc in each sc around.

Rnd 3: Work even in sc—8 sc.

Rnd 4: (Sc in next sc, 2 sc in next sc) 4 times—12 sc.

Rnd 5: Work even in sc.

Rnd 6: (Sc in next sc, 2 sc in next sc) 6 times—18 sc.

Rnd 7: Work even in sc.

Rnd 8: (Sc in next sc, 2 sc in next sc) 9 times—27 sc.

Rnds 9-14: Work even in sc.

Rnd 15: (Sc in next sc, work next 2 sc tog) 9 times—18 sc.

Rnd 16: Work even in sc.

Rnd 17: Work 2 sc tog around. Stuff head; sew up opening. Sew head to neck.

Ear (make 2): Ch 7.

Row 1: Sc in 2nd ch from hook and in each remaining ch—6 sc. Ch 1, turn each row.

Row 2: 2 sc in first sc, sc across, 2 sc in last sc—8 sc.

Rows 3 and 4: Work even in sc.

Rows 5 and 6: Work 2 sc tog, sc across to last 2 sc, work last 2 sc tog—4 sc.

Row 7: Work even in sc. End off (upper edge of ear).

Cut pink felt same shape as ear. If velour is used, add ¼″ all around for turning under. Sew ear lining to ear. Sew ears to head, cupping slightly.

HAUNCHES AND LEGS: Beg at center of haunch, ch 2.

Rnd 1: 6 sc in 2nd ch from hook.

Rnd 2: 2 sc in each sc around.

Rnd 3: (Sc in next sc, 2 sc in next sc)—18 sc.

Rnd 4: Work even in sc.

Rnd 5: (Sc in next sc, 2 sc in next sc) 9 times—27 sc.

Rnd 6: Work even in sc. Ch 6 for leg. Sc in 2nd ch from hook and in each of next 4 ch, sc in 4 sc on edge of haunch. Ch 1, turn. Work 3 more rows on these 9 sc. End off.

For other leg, after finishing haunch, ch 1, turn. Work 4 sc on haunch, ch 6, for leg. Work as for first leg. Stuff haunch; roll leg, stuff and sew up, leaving toe end open. Sew to body with leg sticking out to front.

ARMS (make 2): Ch 7, sl st in first ch to form ring. Ch 1, sc in each ch around. Work 2 more rnds even on 7 sc. Dec 1 sc on next rnd. Work 1 rnd even —6 sc. Dec 1 sc on next rnd—5 sc.

Form Elbow: Sc in first 2 sc. Ch 1, turn. Work 1 row even on 2 sc. Ch 1, turn.

Next Row: Sc in 2 sc, sc in each of 3 sc on rnd. Work 4 rnds even on 5 sc. End off. Stuff; sew to toy, leaving wrist end open.

FINISHING: Trace patterns for hands, feet, and palms. Cut out paper patterns. Using patterns, cut from grey felt two hands, two feet, and four palms. Glue palms to feet and hands stuffing lightly with yarn scraps. Insert feet in leg openings and hands in arm openings; sew securely.

For eyes, cut two ½″-diameter blue felt circles. Cut three ¼″-diameter black felt circles for pupils and nose. Glue in place.

For mouth, take one long stitch with embroidery floss and secure. For whiskers, thread needle with waxed thread; run needle back and forth through nose several times, leaving long loops on each side and taking small stitches at side of nose to secure whiskers; cut through loops.

Mother Mouse's Clothes

1. Dress. Cut one 5″ × 18″ scrap for skirt and one 2¼″ × 5½″ piece for top. Stitch ends of skirt together for back seam. Gather top edge. Fit on toy under arms; mark hem. Hem bottom edge. Adjust gathers along top edge; sew skirt to toy at underarms.

Fold each long edge of top piece, wrong sides together, to center of strip; press. Make a narrow hem along each short end. Wrap top around neck, seam side down, and bring short ends together at front. Sew ends to skirt top at front, sew back to skirt top at back.

2. Cap. Using pinking shears, cut 3½″-diameter circle of fabric for cap. Gather ¾″ in from edge, pull up, stuff center, and sew to head.

3. Apron. For apron, hem sides of 6″-long piece of eyelet trimming. Gather top raw edge to length of 2″, sew to center of 20″ length of ribbon. Tie ribbon ends into bow at mouse's back.

Father Mouse's Clothes

1. Vest. Trace pattern for vest, place pattern on toy, adjust to fit, and cut out. Place pattern on vest fabric, draw around outline. Cut out vest ¼″ outside of marked line. Similarly, cut vest piece from lining material. Cut out armholes on lining material. Stitch vest to lining, right sides together, leaving ¼″ seam allowances and an opening at bottom. Turn to right side; press. Close opening. Make four slashes through lining armholes into each armhole of outer fabric from center to outer edge of armhole. Turn fabric to inside of vest over lining. Trim to ⅛″ and hem down. Place vest on toy. Turn down lapels. Sew button to overlapped fronts below lapels.

2. Dickey and necktie. For dickey, cut 2″ square of fabric. Turn under one edge; gather slightly and sew to neck. Tuck dickey inside vest.

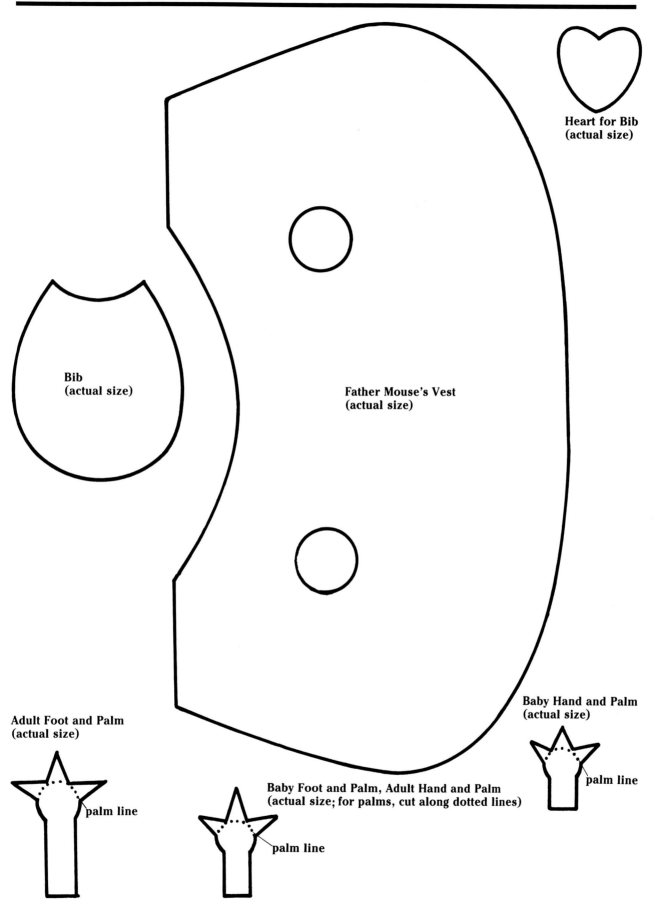

Heart for Bib
(actual size)

Bib
(actual size)

Father Mouse's Vest
(actual size)

Adult Foot and Palm
(actual size)

palm line

Baby Foot and Palm, Adult Hand and Palm
(actual size; for palms, cut along dotted lines)

palm line

Baby Hand and Palm
(actual size)

palm line

For tie, cut two 1¾" × 2½" pieces of fabric. Join them, right sides together around edges, leaving opening for turning. Turn to right side; press. Cut another ¾" square of matching fabric. Fold under two opposite sides of piece; wind folded strip around center of tie to form bow tie; sew ends together. Sew tie to dickey.

Baby Mouse

BABY MOUSE'S BODY: Work as for Mouse through rnd 4.

Rnds 5-10: Work even in sc.

Rnd 11: (Sc in each of 7 sc, work 2 sc tog) 3 times—24 sc.

Rnd 12: Work even.

Rnd 13: (Sc in each of 4 sc, work 2 sc tog) 4 times—20 sc.

Rnd 14: Work even.

Rnd 15: (Sc in each of 2 sc, work 2 sc tog) 5 times—15 sc.

Rnd 16: Work even.

Rnd 17: (Sc in next sc, work 2 sc tog) 5 times—10 sc.

Rnd 18: Work even.

Rnd 19: Work 2 sc tog around. End off. Stuff; leave neck open.

HEAD: Beg at tip of nose, ch 2.

Rnd 1: 5 sc in 2nd ch from hook.

Rnd 2: Work even.

Rnd 3: 2 sc in each sc around.

Rnd 4: Work even.

Rnd 5: (Sc in next sc, 2 sc in next sc) 5 times—15 sc.

Rnds 6 and 7: Work even.

Rnd 8: (Sc in each of 2 sc, 2 sc in next sc) 5 times—20 sc.

Rnds 9-11: Work even.

Rnd 12: (Sc in each of 2 sc, work 2 sc tog) 5 times—15 sc.

Rnd 13: Work even. Stuff.

Rnd 14: Sc in next sc, (work 2 sc tog) 7 times. End off. Sew up opening. Sew head to neck.

EAR (make 2): Ch 5.

Row 1: Sc in 2nd ch from hook and in each remaining ch—4 sc. Ch 1, turn each row.

Row 2: 2 sc in first sc, sc in 2 sc, 2 sc in last sc.

Row 3 and 4: Work even.

Rows 5 and 6: Work first 2 and last 2 sc tog each row. End off. Line ears as for Adult Mouse. Sew on.

LEG (make 2): Ch 6.

Row 1: Sc in 2nd ch from hook and in each remaining ch. Ch 1, turn each row.

Rows 2 and 3: Sc in each sc. End off. Roll up; sew long edges tog. Sew to body.

ARM (make 2): Work as for leg working only 2 rows.

TAIL: Make a ch about 6" long. Sew to lower back of body.

FINISHING: Finish as for Mother Mouse, cutting features slightly smaller.

Baby's Clothes

1. Diaper. Cut 3½" × 6" piece for diaper, narrowing it slightly at center. Pin on each side around baby with safety pin.

2. Bib. Using pattern, cut two bib pieces. Stitch, right sides together, leaving top open. Turn to right side, press. Turn in open edges, and sew opening closed. Sew top of bib to center of 15" length of ribbon. Cut out heart-shaped piece of plain fabric. Glue to center of bib. Tie bib on baby mouse.

Farmgirl, Farm Animals, and Barn Tote

Amuse a youngster with any or all of these cheerful inhabitants of a make-believe farm. The quilted tote is just the right size for carrying them all together.

Farmgirl Doll

SIZE: 13½″ tall.

MATERIALS: Fabric: ⅜ yard 36″-wide tightly woven pink cotton; ¼ yard 36″-wide polka dot print; about 10″ square scrap of solid color cotton; scraps of white cotton knit (old sock will do); scraps of black vinyl. Matching sewing thread. Narrow rickrack. Six-strand embroidery floss in light and dark brown and

red. Polyester fiberfill for stuffing. Brown knitting yarn. Sobo glue.

1. Making the patterns and cutting body sections. Enlarge patterns by copying designs onto paper ruled in 1″ squares; complete half and quarter patterns indicated by dash lines. From pink cotton, cut two body pieces and four legs (reverse pattern for two legs) adding ¼″ all around each piece for seam allowances.

2. The face. With carbon paper between pattern and right side of one body piece, transfer facial features by tracing pattern with hard-lead pencil. Using outline stitches, make outlines of eyes and eyebrows with dark brown floss, nose and chin with light brown floss, and mouth with red floss. Using dark brown floss and satin stitches fill in pupils. See *Embroidery Stitches* at back of book.

3. Assembling body. Stitch body sections right sides together, leaving bottom open. Clip into seam allowances at curves; turn right side out and stuff. For each leg, stitch two corresponding pieces right sides together, leaving opening at top. Clip curve; turn right side out and stuff.

With raw edges of body turned in, pin legs between front and back of body with leg seams at front and back. Slip-stitch opening closed, catching legs.

4. The hair. Cut sixty 12″-long strands of knitting yarn and ten 17″-long strands. Drape all strands across head from side to side with the longer strands at forehead. Stitch across center of strands from front to back of head. For little curl in center of forehead, loop one long strand a couple of times and tack. Trim all shorter strands to shoulder length. Bring longer front strands around sides to back and tack at center back of head; trim. Glue hair to head where necessary.

5. The romper. Cut two pieces from polka dot print, adding ¼″ all around for seam allowances. Slash down to cross-line on one piece only (back). Make narrow hem around neck, sleeves, and leg openings. Fold in half at shoulders, right sides together; stitch underarm, sides, and crotch seams. Turn right side out. Sew rickrack around neck, sleeve, and leg openings. Slip garment on doll. Gather sleeve and leg openings indicated by dotted lines on pattern. Turn in edges and slip-stitch back opening closed.

6. The skirt. Cut skirt from solid color fabric. Make ¼″ hem along all raw edges. Cut two pockets from polka dot print, each 1¾″ square. Turn under all raw edges ¼″. Stitch rickrack across one edge of each, for top of pocket. Stitch a pocket to skirt along sides

and bottom, at each end of skirt as indicated by short dash lines on pattern. Tuck a scrap of fabric in one pocket for handkerchief; tack. Using contrasting color thread, sew running stitches around entire skirt. Gather at waist; stitch to romper around doll.

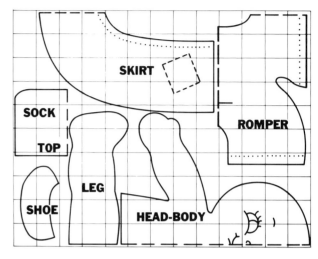

Farmgirl Pattern   **Each square = 1″**

7. The socks and shoes. Cut two socks from white cotton knit or old sock. Fold each sock in half crosswise, right sides facing and sew, leaving ⅛″ seam allowances and the top edge open. Turn right side out and slip on doll's foot. Turn top edge under and slip-stitch top of sock to doll's leg.

Cut four shoes from vinyl, reversing pattern for two. Match two corresponding pieces right sides together. Sew around front, bottom, and back leaving ⅛″ seam allowances. Turn right side out. Slip onto foot with a bit of glue to hold in place. Repeat for other shoe.

8. The hair bow. Cut 4¾″ × 18″ strip from polka dot print. Fold strip in half lengthwise, right sides together. Stitch all raw edges together, leaving ¼″ seam allowances and an opening for turning. Clip corners and turn. Turn edges of opening under and slip-stitch closed. Fold strip in thirds forming bow. Cut another ¾″ × 2½″ fabric strip. Fold long raw edges under. Gather center of bow with smaller strip. Tack ends under bow. Stitch bow to top of head.

Barn Tote

SIZE: About 10¼" × 13".

MATERIALS: 1 yard 36"- to 45"-wide cotton denim fabric. Small amounts of solid and print fabrics. Dacron or cotton batting for padding. ½ yard 18"-wide Stitch Witchery® fusible web. White sewing thread.

1. Making the patterns. Enlarge patterns by copying on paper ruled in 1" squares. Solid heavier lines indicate individual pieces; short dash lines indicate where pieces are overlapped. Fine lines indicate stitching.

2. Cutting the fabric. From denim, cut two fronts and two backs, each 10¾" × 13½". Cut two pieces of batting the same size.

Using patterns, cut out two of each appliqué piece from various fabrics. Cut out fusible web for each appliqué piece.

3. The appliqué. Position and pin fabric pieces on right side of one front and one back denim rectangle with fusible web between. With iron, press appliqués in place, removing pins as you press; follow directions that come with web.

Place a plain and an appliquéd denim section wrong sides together with a layer of batting between them, and, using white thread, machine stitch along all fine lines.

4. The boxing strips. From denim, cut four 1¾" × 10¾" boxing strips for the sides, and two 1¾" × 13½" strips for the bottom. Cut batting same size. Place batting between wrong sides of each pair of matching strips and stitch together, sewing a wavy line through center of strip with white thread.

All seams of tote are to be bound. Therefore, sew front and back together with right sides out. Pin side and bottom boxing strips to bag front; sew, leaving ¼" seam allowances. Stitch back of bag to other edge of boxing. Stitch ends of bottom boxing to side boxing strips.

5. The binding. To bind seams, cut 1¼"-wide bias strips from denim; piece to make long enough to encase raw edges of tote. With right sides together, sew length of strip to one side of seam. Fold strip over raw edge of

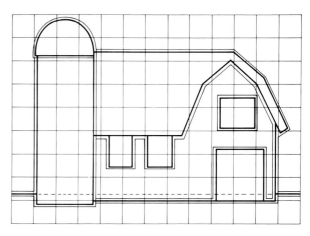

Barn Pattern   **Each square = 1"**

seam; fold raw edge of strip under ¼"; slip-stitch in place. Repeat for all raw edges. Bind open top edges of tote in same manner.

6. The handles. Cut two 3½" × 14" pieces. Fold long edges to center and then fold in half lengthwise; press. Topstitch along open lengthwise edges of each handle.

Turn under ends of each handle. Machine stitch both ends of one handle to front of tote 4½" apart and centered. Repeat for back handle.

Barnyard Animals

MATERIALS: Small amounts of cotton print fabric and terry cloth. Dacron polyester for stuffing. Small amount of yarn for horse and pig. Bits of felt in colors indicated in individual directions. Small amounts red and black six-strand embroidery floss. Small bell for sheep. White sewing thread. Three yellow pompons from ball fringe for chicks. All-purpose white glue. Black felt-tipped pen.

General Directions

1. Making the patterns and cutting the fabric. Enlarge patterns by copying on paper ruled in 1" squares. For each animal cut two complete bodies and two bottom gussets indicated by dot-dash line (except for Hen), from cotton fabric. Add ¼" for seam allowances on all fabric pieces. For Hen, place dash line of gusset pattern on fold of doubled fabric.

2. Assembling the bodies. With right sides together, sew one bottom gusset to each body around legs and bottom of body, leaving straight edge of gusset open. Sew bodies right sides together, from A, around head and back, to B, leaving gusset open. Follow individual directions for nose on pig and muzzle on sheep. Turn right side out; stuff. Slip-stitch gusset opening closed.

For pig and dog ears, and hen wings, cut four of each from fabric; stitch right sides together in pairs, leaving small opening at base. Turn right side out. Turn in raw edges and whip together.

To embroider features, use full six strands of floss in needle and refer to *Embroidery Stitches* at back of book. Using black floss, embroider eyes in satin stitch. Make one straight stitch in red floss for all mouths, except sheep and chickens. Follow individual instructions for finishing.

Pig: Cut pink felt circle for nose. Sew body and ears following General Directions; leave nose area open. Glue nose in place after pig is stuffed. Sew ear to each side of head as indicated on pattern. Mark nostrils with pen. For tail, thread tapestry needle with 12″ length of pink yarn; curl end around pencil several times; then push needle between yarn fibers of each curl. Tack to rear. Embroider features on each side of head.

Dog: For collar, cut strip ⅛″ × 2¾″ from brown felt. Sew body and ears, following General Directions. Embroider eyes on each side of head; satin stitch nose with black floss. Glue collar around dog's neck as shown.

Horse: Cut two ears from white felt. Sew body together following General Directions. Tack ears to head as indicated on pattern. Embroider eyes and mouth on each side of head; satin stitch nostrils in red floss. Cut sixteen 4″ lengths of brown yarn; for mane, stitch center of strands along seam of head from ears to back of neck. Cut three 1″ lengths

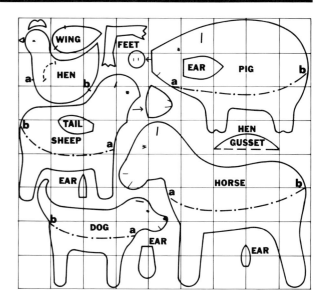

Farm Animals Patterns   Each square = 1″

of yarn; stitch centers on top of head as shown. Cut five 6″ lengths for tail. Tie in center and tack center to rear.

Sheep: Cut body and one tail from terry cloth; cut two ears, two muzzles and one tail from white felt. Sew muzzle to each side of body before stitching bodies together. Embroider nose and mouth on each side of head in straight stitches with black floss. Tie bell to piece of yarn around neck. For tail, sew terry cloth and felt pieces right sides together. Turn right side out and tack to rear.

Hen: Cut comb from red felt, beak and feet from yellow felt. Sew body pieces together from A, around head, back and tail, to B. Stitch gusset to both sides of bottom, leaving an opening. Turn right side out and stuff; slip-stitch opening closed. Tack wings in place as indicated on pattern. Glue comb, beak, and feet to body.

Chickens: For each chick, trim into center of pompon to form head. Cut beak from yellow-orange felt; glue to head. Mark eyes with pen.

Assorted Nursery Accessories

Cross-stitch, appliqué, lace, and paint turn ordinary accoutrements of the nursery into eye-catching accessories that make welcome gifts for the newborn.

Basket

EQUIPMENT: Small paintbrush. Old newspapers.

MATERIALS: Wicker basket with handle (the one shown is 13″ × 10″). Lilac spray paint. Blue, light green, pink, and white acrylic paints. Ribbons: ¾ yard ¾″-wide blue grosgrain; 1 yard 1½″-wide white satin.

Place basket on newspapers and cover entire surface with lilac spray paint; let dry. Using paintbrush, decorate basket with acrylic paints as shown, or as desired; let dry. Tie ribbons to handle, as shown.

Book Cover

EQUIPMENT: Tapestry needle. Small embroidery hoop. Masking tape.

MATERIALS: Small photo album or book, about 4½″ × 5¾″. 22-threads-to-the-inch Hardanger cloth; to determine dimensions of piece needed, add 1″ to book height and 4″ to entire book width, measured from front edge around spine to back edge. White cotton fabric, same size as Hardanger cloth. One ball purple pearl cotton #8.

1. Marking and cross-stitching cover.

Bind edges of Hardanger cloth. With wrong side of Hardanger cloth facing out, fit piece around closed book, having ½" extending at top and bottom and 2" at side edges (book is shown on its side in photograph). Turn side margins to inside covers and tape in place. Mark line along top and bottom, ⅛" beyond edges. On one cover, mark 3½" × 4¹¹⁄₁₆" design area on hardanger cloth, centering it with equal margins all around; design can be adjusted in any direction to fit by adding or subtracting ⅝" (width of one heart). Untape piece and baste along marked lines. With right side up, insert Hardanger cloth in hoop. Using one strand pearl cotton in tapestry needle, work design in cross-stitch within outline, following chart for upper right corner of design and referring to *Embroidery Stitches* at back of book. Each symbol on chart represents a cross-stitch worked over two horizontal and two vertical threads. For first stitch, indicated by arrow, count six threads from corner for the three blank squares shown. Repeat hearts as shown, working five across top and bottom and seven down sides, or as many as needed to fill outline.

2. Attaching cover. When embroidery is completed, place Hardanger and white fabric right sides together and raw edges even. Stitch along basting at top and bottom; turn to right side. Fit cover around book, centering design on front. Fold short edges to inside of front and back covers, turn under edges, and slip-stitch closed at top and bottom.

Box

EQUIPMENT: Small embroidery hoop.

MATERIALS: 6¼"-tall and 3½"-wide clear plastic box. 7½" × 9½" piece orange gingham with ¹⁄₁₆" checks. Small amount purple pearl cotton #5. 3¼" × 4¼" piece lightweight cardboard. Orange sewing thread.

1. Cross-stitch. For cross-stitch see *Embroidery Stitches* at back of book. With short edges of fabric at top and bottom, measure 3½" in and down from upper right corner for placement of first stitch, indicated

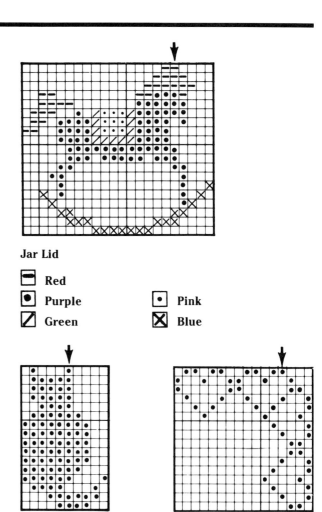

Jar Lid

- ▬ Red
- ● Purple
- ⁄ Green
- · Pink
- ✕ Blue

Box

Book Cover

on chart by arrow, and mark with pin; each stitch is worked over a block of four checks. Insert fabric in hoop. With one strand pearl cotton in embroidery needle, follow chart to work cat in cross-stitch.

2. Finishing embroidery. When embroidery is completed, center piece over cardboard and fold excess fabric to back of board. Slip-stitch opposite edges together in back, turning top raw edge under ¼". Place in box, as shown.

Jar Lid

EQUIPMENT: Compass. Small embroidery hoop.

MATERIALS: 5½" tall apothecary jar with 3"-diameter knob-shaped lid. 6½" square orange gingham with ¹⁄₁₆" checks. 24" length

¼"-wide orange satin ribbon. Batting. Pearl cotton #8: scraps of purple, blue, red, green, pink. 20" length 1"-wide pre-gathered white eyelet trim. Rubber band.

1. Cross-stitch. Using compass, mark a 6"-diameter circle in center of orange gingham on right side of fabric; do not cut out. Measure 2¾" in and 2½" down from upper right corner of gingham for placement of first stitch, indicated on chart by arrow, and mark with pin; each stitch is worked over one check. Insert fabric in hoop. With one strand pearl cotton in embroidery needle, follow chart and color key to work rocking horse in cross-stitch. See *Embroidery Stitches* at back of book.

2. Finishing lid. Cut out circle. With right sides facing and raw edges even, stitch eyelet trim in place around edge of fabric; press raw edges to inside. Cut 5"-diameter circle from batting. Center batting and embroidery over lid; secure with rubber band; tie orange ribbon over rubber band.

Bottle Covers

MATERIALS: Assorted bottles and jars containing baby powder, lotion, etc. Lilac gingham with ⅛" checks (see directions for amounts). ¾"-wide lace trim, as needed. Small round elastic, as needed.

1. Making cover(s). Cut fabric to fit around bottle or jar, adding ½" to circumference and 1½" to length (omitting cap or lid). Fold fabric in half, right sides together; stitch lengthwise edges together leaving ¼" seam allowances. At top and bottom, turn edge under ⅛", then ¼", topstitch in place along inner folds leaving 1" opening to insert elastic; turn to right side. Using safety pin, lace elastic through openings at top and bottom; pull to gather; knot ends, slip-stitch openings closed.

2. Trimming cover. Put cover on bottle or jar, mark position of shoulder on fabric, remove cover, stitch lace around cover at shoulder.

Door Sign

MATERIALS: 8" × 10" lilac gingham with ¹⁄₁₆" check. 4" × 9" piece blue calico Batting. Lilac sewing thread. ¾ yard ⅜"-wide pink ribbon.

1. Making patterns. Using pencil and ruler, draw lines across pattern, connecting grid lines. Enlarge patterns by copying designs on paper ruled in 1" squares. Make a separate pattern for each piece.

2. Marking and cutting fabric. Using dressmaker's carbon and dry ball-point pen, mark pieces on wrong side of fabrics, placing them ½" apart and ½" from fabric edge: Mark two clouds on lilac gingham, reversing pattern for second piece; mark letters on blue calico; cut out pieces, adding ¼" seam allowances. Use patterns to cut same-size piece of batting for each section.

3. Assembling cloud. Pin clouds right sides together with raw edges even, and batting on top. Stitch together, leaving ¼" seam allowances and bottom curve open for turning. Turn to right side. Turn raw edges along opening under ¼"; slip-stitch closed.

4. The appliqué and trim. Referring to *How to Appliqué* directions at back of book and following photograph and pattern for placement, pin letters and their matching batting pieces to cloud. Machine-appliqué pieces in place.

Tie small bow in center of pink ribbon; stitch free ends to back of cloud, as shown.

Door Sign   **Each square = 1"**

Infant's Yo-yo Quilt and Pillow Set

Traditional yo-yo circles joined in concentric circles make colorful additions to an infant or toddler's bedroom in the form of a matching pillow and quilt.

Infant's Yo-yo Quilt

SIZE: Finished quilt size, approximately 38″ diameter. Finished pillow size, approximately 18½″ diameter.

EQUIPMENT: Compass. Thin, stiff cardboard.

MATERIALS: For yo-yo patches, scraps of solid and print lightweight cotton fabrics, in colors desired. 1⅓ yards 36″-wide printed cotton fabric for backing. 1⅓ yards 36″-wide light-colored cotton for lining, such as pre-shrunk, unbleached muslin or solid broadcloth. 1⅝ yards 45″-wide yellow-checked gingham for ruffle. Matching sewing thread. Strong sewing thread for making yo-yo's. Dacron polyester batting.

The Yo-yos

For patterns, cut several 3¾″ circles from cardboard; replace patterns as edges become worn from use. Using pencil, trace pattern outlines on wrong side of fabrics; cut circles from fabric. Mark a line with tailor's chalk on right side of each fabric circle ¼″ from edge (a 3¼″ cardboard circle would be helpful in marking).

Holding fabric circle right side up, turn ¼″ of fabric to back along marked line; baste. Using doubled thread in needle, sew around circle ⅛″ from edge with small even running stitches; do not backstitch as you sew. Gather circle until small hole is formed in center and secure thread with several small backstitches. Flatten the puff to make a round patch. Patches should measure approximately 1¾″ diameter. You will need total of about 422 yo-yo patches: 361 for the quilt and 61 for the pillow.

The Quilt

1. The backing, lining, and ruffle. Cut one 33½″ circle each from printed backing fabric and solid lining fabric. Cut a piece of batting the same size. From checked gingham, cut six 6″ × 45″ strips. Connect strips at short ends, right sides together, leaving ¼″ seam allowances. Fold in half lengthwise and sew with gathering stitches ¼″ inside raw lengthwise edges; gather to make 3″-wide ruffle that will fit circumference of backing, plus ¼″.

Place backing on flat surface right side up. Pin ruffling around circle aligning raw edges and adjusting gathers so they are evenly distributed. Baste ruffle to backing around edge. Baste batting to lining fabric. Pin lining on top of ruffling with right side down and ruffle inside. Stitch ¼″ inside edge, leaving a 12″ opening. Turn to right side. Slip-stitch opening closed. Baste backing, batting, lining together through all layers.

2. Quilting. With tailor's chalk and ruler, draw diagonal lines from left to right, then from right to left, leaving a 2″ space between. Quilt by hand or machine through all layers along marked lines with short, even running stitches.

3. Attaching yo-yos. Complete quilt by attaching yo-yo patch layer as follows. Arrange yo-yo patches as desired in circular rows on completed quilt. Outside row of yo-yo's should overlap ruffling by about ½″. To sew together place two adjacent patches right sides together; make tiny overcast stitches through edges of one side for about ¼″. Complete circular rows, beginning with outer edge and working toward center: connect adjacent rows with tiny slip-stitches. Attach completed layer of yo-yo patches to quilt by slip-stitching around outer edge and tacking to lining at regular intervals.

The Pillow

1. Cutting the fabric. Cut one 14½″ circle each from printed backing fabric and solid lining fabric. Cut a piece of batting the same size. From checked gingham, cut three 6″ × 45″ strips. Connect strips, fold, and gather raw edges as for quilt ruffle.

2. Assembling pillow. Baste circle of batting to wrong side of backing fabric. Quilt with diagonal stitches as for quilt. Lay backing right side up on flat surface. Pin ruffling around edge and baste as for quilt. Attach pillow lining as for quilt lining, leaving 6″ opening. Turn to right side. Stuff with batting; slip-stitch opening closed. Complete pillow by attaching yo-yo patch layer same as for quilt.

A Trio of Scenic Appliqués for a Youngster's Tunic, Pillow, and Wall-Pocket Organizer

All three of the landscapes that adorn these projects are machine appliquéd and easily assembled. The tunic is designed solely for a girl, but the pillow and wall pockets are suitable for either sex.

Wall-Pocket Organizer

SIZE: 11¼″ square.

EQUIPMENT: Compass.

MATERIALS: Cotton fabric: 8″ × 12¼″ solid blue piece for sky; 12¼″ square small print for backing; four different print fabrics for mountain pockets, each 12¼″ wide and at least 8½″ deep; 2½″ square scrap of gold print for sun, Sewing thread in green and gold. Two ½″ × 2¼″ white felt strips for hanging loops.

1. Making the patterns. Enlarge pattern by copying design on paper ruled in 1″ squares; short dash line indicates where piece is overlapped; dotted lines indicate decorative stitching for pocket separations.

2. Marking and cutting out fabric. Using dressmaker's carbon and tracing wheel (or dry ball-point pen), transfer the outline of the four separate mountain pockets to four different fabrics, extending each one to bottom of pattern; transfer dotted lines. Draw a second line around first for ½″ seam allowance. Cut out pieces along outer lines.

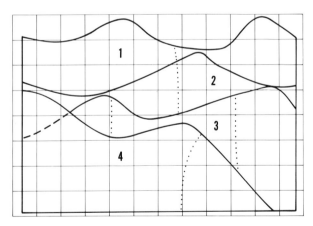

Wall Pockets Each square = 1″

3. Assembling wall pockets. On each pocket, press seam allowance of top edge to wrong side; if necessary, clip curves so fabric will lie flat. Using green thread, topstitch along curves with zigzag stitch. Press pockets flat.

With all fabrics facing right side up and keeping all straight edges even, form pocket separations in this order, using zigzag stitch and green thread: Pin pocket (2) to top of pocket (1); stitch along dotted line, continuing to bottom edge. Pin pocket (4) to top of pocket (3); stitch along dotted line of (4) only. With pocket (3) against pocket (2), stitch along dotted line, being careful not to stitch through pockets (1) or (4). With all side and bottom edges even, baste ⅛″ from those edges to hold pockets together.

4. Hanging loops. Fold felt strips in half and baste to top edge of backing fabric on right side, 1½″ in from either side and with strip ends extending over edge of backing.

5. Joining pockets to backing. With right sides together, pin pockets to bottom portion of backing. Baste carefully about ⅛″ from raw edges on bottom and sides keeping all edges even. With right sides together, pin sky to top edge of backing fabric. Baste carefully about ⅛″ from raw edges on top and sides, keeping edges even.

Stitch around edges through all thicknesses leaving ½″ seam allowances. Trim corners. Turn right side out through sky opening; push out corners with a pointed object. Press flat.

Using compass, mark 2½″ diameter sun on gold print fabric. Referring to *How to Appliqué* section at back of book, cut out sun and appliqué by machine to sky, using matching thread, fine-stitch length, and #3 width on machine.

Tack top edge of pocket (1) through sky and backing fabrics at dotted line.

Scenic Pillow

SIZE: 12″ square.

MATERIALS: 13″ square blue cotton for front; about 12 small pieces of assorted fabrics for appliqués; 13″ × 17″ piece corduroy for back. Sewing thread to match fabrics. ⅜ yard 36″-wide muslin for inner pillow. Fiberfill for stuffing.

1. Making the pattern. Enlarge pattern by copying design on paper ruled in 1″ squares. Heavy solid lines indicate appliqués; dotted lines indicate stitching only.

2. The appliqué. Trace each separate part of appliqué design (omitting sky). Referring to

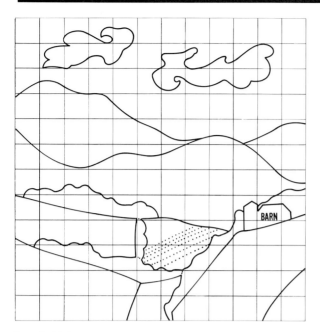

Scenic Pillow   **Each square = 1″**

How to Appliqué section at back of book, cut appliqués from assorted fabrics, adding ¼″ seam allowances; on those pieces that end at side and bottom edges of pillow, add ½″ for pillow seam allowance. Use purple for mountains, green for trees, stripes for planted fields (see photograph).

Pin and straight-stitch all appliqué pieces except for barn shape, on blue front piece, placing them as indicated on pattern and matching outer raw edges. Set machine for close zigzag stitches and complete appliquéing as directed. On one piece of fabric use irregular zigzag stitching to indicate growing crops (dotted lines). Stitch on barn shape last.

3. Pillow back. Cut corduroy into two 8½″ × 13″ pieces. Turn one long edge of each piece under ½″ and topstitch to make hem. Overlap hemmed edges of both pieces, with right sides of both facing up, to make 13″ square and tack together at overlapped side edges. Place appliquéd front piece and back pieces right sides together and raw edges flush. Pin, then stitch edges together leaving ½″ seam allowances. Clip corners and turn to right side. Push out corners.

4. Inner pillow. Cut two 13½″ squares from muslin. Sew edges together on all sides, leaving ¼″ seam allowances and a 6″ opening

for turning at center of one side. Turn to right side. Stuff pillow fully. Turn under edges of opening and slip-stitch closed. Insert inner pillow into appliquéd pillow through back.

Child's Tunic

SIZE: 2-4.

MATERIALS: ¼ yard 44″- to 45″-wide solid-color pinwale corduroy. ½ yard 44″- to 45″-wide printed cotton fabric. Closely woven cotton print fabric scraps for appliqués. Matching threads.

1. Making the patterns. Enlarge pattern by copying design on paper ruled in 1″ squares; complete back half of tunic by flipping pattern at shoulder dash lines and using curving dot-dash line for correct neckline shape.

2. Marking and cutting the fabric. Mark complete outline of tunic on wrong side of corduroy, cut out tunic, adding ¼″ around all

Child's Tunic   **Each square = 1″**

edges and neckline for seam allowances. Make a separate pattern for each appliqué piece; dash lines indicate where pieces overlap. Referring to *How to Appliqué* section at back of book, cut appliqués from various print fabrics.

3. The appliqué. Referring to pattern for placement, pin appliqués in position on tunic front in numerical order, aligning outer raw edges. Straight-stitch and trim, following directions. Set zigzag machine to fine-stitch length and #3 width. Stitch around inner lines of all appliqués, using matching threads.

4. The lining. With right sides together, pin tunic piece to lining fabric. Cut lining fabric to same shape as tunic.

Using a regular machine stitch, stitch around neckline. Clip into seam allowances at ½″ intervals and to point of front neckline V, being careful not to cut into stitching. Pull lining through neckline so that both the tunic fabric and the lining fabric are right side out. Press neckline flat.

5. The ties. Cut four 1″-wide 10″-long strips of lining fabric. Fold strips in half lengthwise, right sides together. Stitch close to open lengthwise edges and across one end. Trim seam allowances and pull ties through to right side. Push corners out with pointed object and press flat. Pin ties to corduroy tunic only, aligning raw edges.

6. Finishing the tunic. Turn garment again so that right sides of tunic and lining are facing; pin bottom and sides together as far up as neckline. Stitch down one side, across bottom, and up other side, leaving ¼″ seam allowances and being careful not to catch finished tie ends. Repeat on other side of tunic. Clip corners to eliminate bulk. Turn tunic right side out and push corners out with a pointed object.

At unstitched shoulder area, turn ¼″ to inside on both tunic and lining, and press. Topstitch ¼″ from edge around entire outside edge of tunic, matching bobbin thread to lining fabric and top thread to tunic fabric.

Animal Collages for a Wall

This trio of a giraffe, lion, and cat can be quickly assembled with some glue and a minimum of stitching. Individually, or together, they would make a welcome gift for any child.

SIZES: Lion, 9½″ × 12″. Giraffe, 7″ × 16½″. Cat, 13″ × 16¾″.

EQUIPMENT: Straight edge. Mat knife. Square.

MATERIALS: Small amounts of fabrics in prints, checks and solids, and corduroy, wool or felt for designs, backgrounds and frames, as desired. Sewing thread. Bits of black embroidery floss and fine brown yarn. Lace and embroidered edgings for lion and giraffe. Sobo glue. Stiff cardboard for backing and frames. See individual directions for specific materials.

General Directions

1. The collages. Enlarge patterns by copying designs on paper ruled in 1″ squares. Short dash lines indicate overlapping pieces. Using patterns, cut out each part of each design from fabrics specified in individual directions.

Cut backing cardboard and background fabric to required size. Arrange all fabric parts of designs on background fabric; fasten pieces in place with light dabs of glue. Stitch pieces and embroider pictures following individual directions and *Embroidering Stitches* section at back of book. Glue background fabric to backing cardboard.

2. The frames. Using metal straight edge, mat knife, and square, cut cardboard frame to size indicated in individual directions. Cut out center opening of frame. Cut fabric for frame 1″ larger all around than cardboard; cut out center opening 1″ smaller than cardboard opening. Center and glue fabric over surface of frame; turn outer edges to back and glue in place. For center opening, slash into fabric at corners to cardboard. Turn fabric to back and glue.

Giraffe

1. The background and giraffe body.
Cut 6¾″ × 16″ piece from cardboard and brown and white polka dot background fabric. Cut giraffe parts from yellow gingham, and

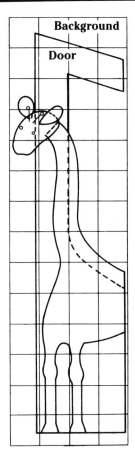

Giraffe Collage

Each square = 1″

doorway shape from brown felt. Glue felt doorway to background fabric as shown on pattern. Then glue lace edging to back of giraffe's neck; glue body to felt, then glue head to end of neck, both ears to front and back of head. Glue cut-out paper or fabric butterflies to background as shown in photograph.

2. Embroidery. Thread brown yarn in embroidery needle; make French knots for eyes and two long, straight stitches with French knot at the outer end of each for horns.

3. The frame. Make 7″ × 16½″ cardboard frame with 4½″ × 13½″ center opening. Follow General Directions to cover frame, using orange-and-white checked fabric.

Lion

1. The background and the lion's body. Cut 8¾″ × 11½″ piece from cardboard backing and brown print background. Cut red felt inner frame.

Cut tail and body from scraps of yellow crushed corduroy. Cut head of white cotton. Thread embroidery needle with fine brown yarn and embroider features onto head as shown using satin stitches for eyes and nose, straight stitches for other features. Tack lengths of yarn to head at X's for whiskers.

All machine stitching is done with a zigzag setting. Sew a lace ruffle and embroidered edging around head. Stitch body to brown print at head, tail and front leg sections. Place the red felt so it frames the print as shown. Stitch around felt frame ¼" from inner edges with wide zigzag stitch.

2. The frame. Make 9¼" × 12" cardboard frame with 7" × 9" center opening. Frame as directed in General Directions using yellow print fabric.

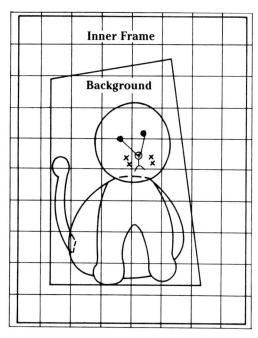

Lion Collage   Each square = 1"

Cat

1. Cutting backing and fabric. Cut 12½" × 16" piece from cardboard backing and 9½" × 12½" piece from light brown background fabric. Cut the eyes and bow from scraps of yellow and white polka dot fabric. Cut lower face, paws, and tail from one brown print; cut entire head and body from another brown print or reverse side of fabric.

Cat Collage   Each square = 1"

2. Assembling cat. All appliqué machine stitching is done with a zigzag setting. Machine stitch eyes to lower part of face.

Embroider pupils, nose, and mouth with black embroidery floss in straight stitches.

Center cat's body on background fabric with tail and small paw piece under body. Stitch fabric in place. Stitch lower face to the head and place on background. Use a little glue and slide part of the bow pieces under the head and body. Stitch head to the body and background. Stitch large paw piece in place.

3. The gingham border. To make gingham borders, cut four 1½"-wide strips of yellow and white checked gingham, two 12½" long and two 11½" long. With right sides together, stitch longer strips of gingham to the 12½"-long sides of the brown fabric, leaving ¼" seam allowances. Press open seam allowances. Then stitch the other two strips to top and bottom edges making sure that the already sewn borders lie flat. Press.

4. The frame. Make 13" × 16½" cardboard frame with a 10½" × 13½" center opening. Cover with orange fabric and frame following General Directions.

Boy-By-the-Sea Wall Hanging

Give the young man in your life something to enjoy on the wall of his room—a fabric landscape full of amusing things to look at, including a boy, the sea, a boat, and a variety of animals—all stitched by machine.

SIZE: 28″ × 19″.

MATERIALS: 16″ × 25″ piece medium-weight, closely-woven cotton for backing. ¾ yard 36″- to 45″-wide calico print cotton for lining and borders. Scraps of fabric in assorted colors, patterns, and textures (as illustrated or as desired) that are suitable for appliqué (such as light blue in plain and dotted Swiss fabrics for sky, brown velour for tree, green prints for leaves and ground, blue denim for overalls, etc.) Sewing threads to match fabrics and in colors indicated below. Red six-strand embroidery floss. Two ¾″-diameter 19″-long wooden dowels.

1. Making the patterns. Enlarge pattern by copying design on paper ruled in 1″ squares. Heavier pattern lines indicate cutting lines. Finer lines indicate lines and areas to be embroidered or stitched by machine.
Trace a separate pattern for each part of design. Sky pieces numbered 1-6 are seamed together. Therefore, add ¼″ seam allowance to lower edge of No. 1 and ¼″ seam allowance to upper and lower edges of the rest. Extend patterns for sky, water, and grass pieces completely across the 16″ width. On hill, water, and grass patterns, which are satin-stitched together, add ⅛″ along lower edge of each where it is overlapped by next piece. Make boy's overall pattern all one piece as indicated by dash lines on pattern. Make shirt and sleeve separate pattern pieces. Make clouds one pattern piece. Continue outer sun circle pattern under cloud and add ⅛″ around inner edge. Continue tree outline under leaves, boy and rabbit. All other pieces are to be cut as given on pattern.

2. Marking the fabric. Transfer outline and fine lines for stitching of each appliqué pattern piece to appropriate fabric, marking on right side of fabric using carbon and dry ball-point pen.

3. Assembling the wall hanging. With right sides facing, sew the six sky sections together leaving ¼″ seam allowances; press seam allowances open. Pin sky to backing fabric with top edges even. Pin sea sections and sections of foreground in place. Following photograph and pattern, pin all other sections

Each square = 1″

into place; baste. Using a medium zigzag satin stitch and matching thread, stitch over edges of pieces. Use a narrow zigzag satin stitch for vein lines of leaves, inner body lines of larger bird and on boy's hat.

Following patterns, mark placement of flower buds on tree. Hand embroider buds using six strands of red floss and straight stitches. (See *Embroidery Stitches* at back of book). Using two strands of appropriate color sewing thread and satin stitches, hand embroider rabbit's features and toes, and bird's features.

Machine embroider remaining fine lines using narrow satin stitches or straight stitches; letter A indicates straight stitching. Follow photograph for colors, or use colors to match and contrast with fabrics being used.

4. Attaching border and lining. From border and lining fabric, cut two 3″ × 25″ pieces and two 3″ × 20″ pieces. Pin 25″ long border along each side length of finished picture, right sides together and edges even. Stitch together leaving ½″ seam allowances. Turn right sides of border out and press open seam allowances. Attach top and bottom borders in the same manner, stitching borders completely across from one side of hanging to the other. Turn right side out and press.

Pin lining piece to picture front, right sides together, and stitch around edges, leaving ½″ seam allowances, a 6″ opening along top for turning and a 1″ opening at one bottom and one top corner on one side to insert dowels. Turn to right side; press edges. Topstitch front and lining together around inside edges of border, ¼″ beyond picture edge. Insert dowels into openings at top and bottom. Slip-stitch all openings closed.

P A R T IV
GENERAL DIRECTIONS

Embroidery Stitches

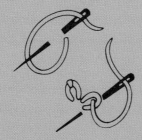

Satin Stitch

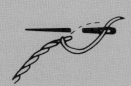

Stem Stitch

French Knot

Lazy Daisy Stitch

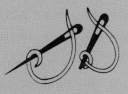

Cross-stitch

Outline Stitch

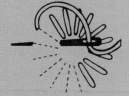

Straight Stitch

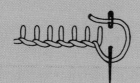

Blanket Stitch

How to Appliqué:

Choose a fabric that is closely woven and firm enough so a clean edge results when the pieces are cut. Cut a pattern piece for each shape out of thin, stiff cardboard, and mark the right side of each pattern piece. Press fabric smooth.

Place cardboard pattern, wrong side up, on wrong side of fabric. Using sharp, hard pencils (light-colored pencil on dark fabric and dark pencil on light fabric), mark the outline on the fabric. When marking several pieces on the same fabric, leave at least ½″ between pieces. Mark a second outline ¼″ outside the design outline. Using matching thread and small stitches, machine-stitch all around design outline, as shown in Figure 1. This makes edge easier to turn and neater in appearance. Cut out the appliqué on the outside line, as shown in Figure 2. For a smooth edge, clip into seam allowance at curved edges and corners. Then turn seam allowance to back, just inside stitching as shown in Figure 3, and press. Pin and baste the appliqué on the background, and slip-stitch in place with tiny stitches, as shown in Figure 4.

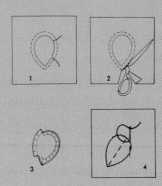

How to Quilt

MAKING THE QUILT TOP

Patterns and Patches. Following individual directions for each quilt, make patterns for patches or appliqués. If making patterns that will be used repeatedly, as for a patchwork quilt, trace master pattern on thin cardboard and cut out with sharp scissors. Because pattern edges become frayed from marking, cut several of each piece. Discard frayed patterns as necessary.

Press all fabric smooth. To determine the straight grain of the fabric, pull a crosswise thread. The line of the thread determines the crosswise grain; threads perpendicular to it run on the lengthwise grain. Place each pattern piece on wrong side of fabric, making sure each piece is placed in correct relationship to the straight grain of fabric as follows.

Squares and oblongs must be placed with the weave of the fabric parallel to edges. Diamond-shaped patches need two sides on straight of the fabric. Right-angle triangles may be cut with two sides on the straight of the goods. For tumbler shapes, the half-pattern should be cut with the fold on the straight of the fabric.

Using light-colored pencil on dark fabric and dark-colored pencil on light fabric, trace around each pattern. When tracing a number of pieces on one fabric, leave space between pieces for seam allowances. For patches and appliqué pieces, you will need ¼″ seam allowance all around each one. **Note:** Yardage requirements in this book are based on careful placement of pattern on fabric. Unless otherwise indicated, patterns should be placed leaving ½″ between two pieces—this will give you the full ¼″ seam allowance that is necessary for each.

Piecing: Align patches right sides together, and hold firmly. Using sewing thread, carefully make tiny running stitches along marked outlines to join. Begin by making a small knot; end with a few backstitches. To avoid bunching of fabric, excess thickness at seams may be trimmed as pieces are assembled.

When joining two bias edges, keep thread just taut enough to prevent seams from stretching.

Unless otherwise indicated, press pieced sections with seams to one side; open seams weaken construction. Compare finished units to make sure all are the same size.

When sewing blocks together, make sure all strips are even with one another.

The size of an allover geometric quilt may be stopped almost anywhere without the danger of throwing the design out of balance.

PREPARING TO QUILT: The quilting design is usually marked on the quilt top after the top is completed but before it is joined to the batting and lining. Select your quilting design carefully to suit the quilt. The designs shown here are some of the more popular and some of the easiest to do. They should be enlarged to three or four times the size shown. Border designs should be traced around the outside, with allover quilting in the center of quilt.

There are two simple methods for transferring a quilting design. The first is to mark the fabric using dressmaker's carbon and a dressmaker's tracing wheel. The second method is to make perforated patterns as follows. Trace the pattern on wrapping paper and, with needle unthreaded, machine-stitch along lines of the design. The design is marked by laying the perforated pattern on the quilt top, rough side down, and rubbing stamping powder or paste through the perforations. Straight lines can be marked with a ruler and tailor's chalk. For very simple quilting that follows the lines of the patchwork, appliqué, or print of fabric, it is not necessary to mark the fabric.

After quilting design has been marked on the quilt top, assemble top, batting, and lining. Cut or piece lining fabric to equal size of quilt top. Place lining, wrong side up, on large flat surface. Place one layer of cotton or Dacron batting on top of lining, smoothing out any bumps or wrinkles. If quilt is planned for warmth, interlining may be thicker. Remember, the thinner the layer of padding, the easier and finer the quilting will be.

Place quilt top right side up on top of batting. Pin all layers together to hold temporarily. Baste generously through all thicknesses. To prevent shifting, first baste on the lengthwise and crosswise grain of the fabric. Then baste diagonally across in two directions and around sides, top, and bottom. **Note:** If quilting is to be done using a quilting hoop, extra care must be taken to keep basting stitches close, so they will hold in place as you change the position of the hoop.

QUILTING: Quilting may be done by hand or on the sewing machine.

When quilting by hand, the quilt may be stretched on a frame or in a quilting hoop (more easily handled and movable). If neither frame nor hoop is used, quilting may be done in the lap over small areas at a time. The first method for making quilting stitches (see below) is best in lap quilting.

Quilting on a Frame. If a frame is used, sew top and bottom edges of lining to the fabric strips which are attached to the long parallel bars of your quilting frame. Using strong thread so that quilt will not pull away from frame when stretched taut, sew securely with several rows of stitches. After quilt is secured in frame, start quilting midway between the long parallel bars of frame and sew toward you. Turn to stitch other side in the same fashion.

Quilting with a Quilting Hoop. Start quilting at the center of the quilt, then work toward outer edges. Pull quilt taut in hoop and move any extra fullness toward the edges. If necessary, cut basting thread as work progresses. As your quilting comes closer to the edge, smaller embroidery hoops may be substituted for the larger quilting hoop, to make sure that fabric will remain taut.

The quilting stitch. A short, even running stitch, usually from five to nine stitches per inch, depending on thickness of the fabrics.

There are two methods of making this stitch. The first is done in two separate motions—first pushing the needle down through the three thicknesses, then pushing it up again close to the first stitch. One hand is

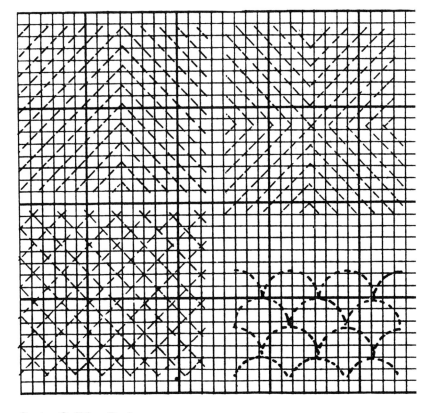

Center Quilting Designs

Border Quilting Designs

always under the quilt to guide the stitch; stitches should be of equal length on both sides of the quilt.

The second method is to take two or three little stitches before pulling the needle through, holding quilt down at quilting line with the thumb of one hand. (Tape this thumb to prevent soreness.)

If you are a beginner, practice quilting a small piece in an embroidery hoop to find the easiest and best way for you to work.

Quilting needle and thread. The usual quilting needle is a short, sharp needle—No. 8 or 9—although some experienced quilters may prefer a longer one. Strong white sewing thread between Nos. 30 and 50 is best. To begin, knot end of thread. Bring needle up through quilt and pull knot through lining so it is embedded in interlining. To end off, make a simple backstitch and run thread through interlining.

Quilting on a machine Machine quilting can be done with or without a quilting foot. When working on a sewing machine, the best quilting patterns to use are sewn on the diagonal or on the bias. Fabric gives a little when on the bias, making it easier to keep the area you are working on flat. Cotton batting should be quilted closely with quilting lines running no more than 2″ apart; Dacron lining may be quilted with the lines no more than 3″ apart.

As a rule, machine quilting is done with a straight stitch. Stitch length control should be set from 6 to 12 per inch. Pressure should be adjusted so that it is slightly heavier than for medium-weight fabrics.

If you are using a scroll or floral design, it is best to use the short open toe of the quilting foot, which allows you to follow the curved lines with accuracy and ease.

TUFTING: If you wish to tuft rather than quilt, use several layers of padding between the top and the lining. Mark evenly spaced points on the top surface with tailor tacks or pins. Thread a candlewick needle with candlewick yarn, or use a large-eyed needle with heavy Germantown yarn or knitting

worsted. Using doubled yarn, push needle from top through layers to back, leaving yarn end on top. Push needle back up again to surface, about ¼″ away. Tie yarn in firm double knot. Clip ends to desired length (at least ½″).

QUILT CARE: Dry clean all fine quilts. If a quilt is washable, you may put it in the automatic washer on a short-wash cycle. Be sure to use only a mild soap or detergent. Do not wring or spin dry. Let quilt drip dry, and do not iron.

How to Needlepoint

To start a needlepoint piece, mark outline of design in center of canvas, leaving at least a 2″ margin around all sides. Bind all raw edges of canvas with masking tape. Find center of canvas by basting a line from center of one edge to the center of opposite edge, being careful to follow a row of spaces. Then baste another line from center of third edge to center of fourth edge. Basting threads will cross at center.

Designs are represented in chart form. Each square on chart represents one mesh on canvas. Each symbol on chart represents a different yarn color.

Cut yarn strands in 18″ lengths. When starting first strand, leave 1″ of yarn on back of canvas and cover it as the work proceeds; your first few stitches will anchor it in place. To end strand or begin a new one, run yarn under a few stitches on back of work; do not make knots. Keep yarn tension firm and even. Stitching tends to twist the working yarn; untwist from time to time, letting yarn and needle hang straight down to unwind. If a mistake is made, run needle under stitch and snip yarn with sharp scissors; do not reuse yarn.

Continental Stitch. The continental stitch can be worked in two different ways, from right to left or from top to bottom, as shown below.

Continental stitch worked horizontally. On each row, start at upper right corner and work across row to left (Drawing 1). Turn work upside down for return row (Drawing 2). Work every row from right to left.

 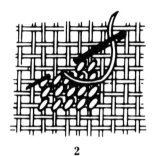

1   2

Continental stitch worked vertically. Work vertical continental stitch from top to bottom as shown in Drawings 1 and 2. Turn work after each row.

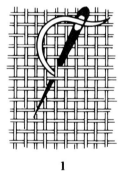 

1   2

How to Knit

Knitting is based on two stitches, the knit stitch and the purl stitch. Many knitted sweaters and accessories can be made with these two stitches alone. Before starting any knitted piece, it is necessary to cast on a certain number of stitches; that is, to place a series of loops on one needle so that you can work your first row of knitting. After you have finished a piece of knitting, it is necessary to bind off the stitches so that they will not ravel.

CASTING ON

There are many ways of casting on stitches. The method shown here is only one of them. It gives you a strong and elastic edge.

Step 1: Allow enough yarn for the number of stitches to be cast on (about ½″ per stitch for lighter weight yarns such as baby yarns, 1″ per stitch for heavier yarns such as knitting worsted, more for bulky yarns on large needles). Make a slip loop on needle, as shown above, and tighten knot gently.

Step 2: Hold needle in right hand with short end of yarn over left thumb. Weave strand that comes from ball through right hand, over index finger, under second, over third and under fourth finger.

Step 3: Bring needle forward to make a loop over left thumb. Insert needle from left to right in loop; bring yarn in right hand under, then over point of needle and draw yarn through loop with tip of needle.

Step 4: Keeping right hand in same position, tighten stitch on needle gently with left hand. You now have 2 stitches on needle. Repeat Steps 3 and 4 for required number of stitches.

KNIT STITCH

Step 1: Hold needle with cast on stitches in left hand and yarn in same position as for casting on in right hand. Insert point of needle from left to right in first stitch.

Step 2: Bring yarn under and over point of right needle.

Step 3: Draw yarn through stitch with point of needle.

Step 4: Allow loop on left needle to slip off needle. Loop on right needle is your first knit stitch. Repeat from Figure 5 in each loop across row. When you have finished knitting one row, place needle with stitches in left hand ready to start next row.

GARTER STITCH

Knit every row to make the garter stitch.

PURL STITCH

To purl, insert needle from right to left in stitch on left needle. Bring yarn over and under point of right needle. Draw yarn back through stitch and allow loop on left needle to slip off needle.

STOCKINETTE STITCH

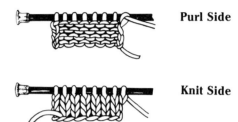

Purl Side

Knit Side

Alternate knit and purl rows to work the stockinette stitch.

BINDING OFF

Knit the first two stitches. Insert left needle from left to right through front of first stitch. Lift first stitch over second stitch and over tip of right needle. One stitch has been bound off, and one stitch remains on right needle. Knit another stitch. Again lift first stitch on right needle over second stitch and off right needle. Continue across until all stitches have been bound off. One loop remains on right needle. Cut yarn, pull end through loop and tighten knot.

INCREASING ONE STITCH

Method 1: Knit 1 stitch in the usual way but do not slip it off left needle. Bring right needle behind left needle, insert it from right to left

in same stitch (called "the back of the stitch") and make another knit stitch. Slip stitch off left needle.

To increase 1 stitch on the purl stitch, purl 1 stitch but do not slip it off left needle. Bring yarn between needles to back, knit 1 stitch in back of same stitch.

Method 2: Pick up horizontal strand between stitch just knitted and next stitch, place it on left needle. Knit 1 stitch in back of this strand, thus twisting it.

Method 3: Place right needle behind left needle. Insert right needle in stitch below next stitch, knit this stitch, then knit stitch above it in the usual way.

```
        KNITTING ABBREVIATIONS

k—knit              psso—pass slip stitch over
p—purl              inc—increase
st—stitch           dec—decrease
sts—stitches        beg—beginning
yo—yarn over        pat—pattern
sl—slip             lp—loop
sk—skip             MC—main color
tog—together        CC—contrasting color
rnd—round           dp—double-pointed
```

How to Crochet

All crochet work begins with a chain, a series of loops made by pulling yarn through a loop on your crochet hook to make a new loop. Many beautiful and intricate patterns can be made in crochet, most of them a variation of a few basic stitches that are illustrated here—chain stitch, single crochet, and slip stitch.

CHAIN STITCH

To make first loop on hook, grasp yarn about 2″ from end between left thumb and index finger. With right hand, lap long strand over short end, forming a loop. Hold loop in place with left thumb and index finger. Grasp hook in right hand, insert hook through loop, catch strand with hook and draw it through loop. Pull end and long strand in opposite directions to close loop around hook.

Step 1: To make your first chain stitch, pass hook under yarn on index finger and catch strand with hook.

Draw yarn through loop on hook. This makes one chain stitch. Repeat last step until you have as many chains as you need. One loop always remains on hook. Practice making all chains uniform.

Step 2: Weave yarn through left hand.

SINGLE CROCHET

Step 1: Insert hook in second chain from hook. Yarn over hook.

Step 2: Draw yarn through chain. Two loops on hook.

Step 3: Yarn over hook. Draw yarn through 2 loops on hook. One single crochet has been made.

Step 4: Work a single crochet in each chain stitch. At end of row, chain 1 and turn work around.

Step 5: Insert hook under both top loops of first stitch, yarn over hook and draw through stitch. Yarn over and through 2 loops on hook. Work a single crochet in same way in each stitch across row.

INCREASING 1 SINGLE CROCHET

To increase 1 single crochet, work 2 stitches in 1 stitch.

DECREASING 1 SINGLE CROCHET

To decrease 1 single crochet, pull up a loop in 1 stitch, pull up a loop in next stitch (3 loops on hook), yarn over hook, draw through all 3 loops at once.

SLIP STITCH

Insert hook in work. Yarn over hook and draw through both the stitch and the loop on hook. The slip stitch makes a firm finishing edge. A single slip stitch is used for joining a chain to form a ring.

TURNING CROCHET WORK

In crochet a certain number of ch sts are needed at the end of each row to bring work into position for the next row. Then work is turned so reverse side is facing the crocheter. For single crochet, chain 1 to turn.

ENDING OFF

When last loop of finished piece is reached, cut yarn end leaving several inches. Pull the end through the loop and thread it through a tapestry needle. Weave the yarn back into the work below the top row of stitches for an inch or two and cut off the excess.

FOLLOWING DIRECTIONS

An asterisk (*) is often used in crochet directions to indicate repetition. For example, when directions read "* 2 dc in next st, 1 dc in next st, repeat from * 4 times" this means to work directions after first * until second * is reached, then go back to first * 4 times more. Work 5 times in all.

When parentheses ( ) are used to show repetition, work directions within parentheses as many times as specified. For example, "(dc, ch 1) 3 times" means to do what is within ( ) 3 times altogether.

"Work even" in directions means to work in same stitch without increasing or decreasing.

CROCHET ABBREVIATIONS	
ch—chain stitch	p—picot
st—stitch	tog—together
sts—stitches	sc—single crochet
lp—loop	sl st—slip stitch
inc—increase	dc—double crochet
dec—decrease	bl—block
rnd—round	sp—space
beg—beginning	pat—pattern
sk—skip	yo—yarn over hook

Have BETTER HOMES AND GARDENS® magazine delivered to your door. For information, write to: MR. ROBERT AUSTIN, P.O. BOX 4536, DES MOINES, IA 50336